LUNATIC, LIAR, or LORD

"*Lunatic, Liar, or Lord* is clear, comprehensive, concise, and convincing: the four things good apologetics should be."

Peter Kreeft
Professor of Philosophy at Boston College

"Wow. What an amazing wellspring of knowledge, encouragement, and conviction Dr. Swafford imparts upon readers in these pages. This wonderful journey packed with wisdom will help you to learn, to grow, and to deepen your faith in Our Eucharistic Lord and the Church."

Emily Wilson Hussem
International speaker and author

"Through the lens of Catholic theology, Dr. Swafford masterfully brings new life to Lewis's classic *Mere Christianity*. At once a survey of Catholic fundamentals, a call to conversion, and a tool for evangelism, *Lunatic, Liar, or Lord* belongs on every believer's bookshelf."

Fr. John Burns
Author of *Lift Up Your Heart*, *Adore*, and *Return*

LUNATIC, LIAR, or LORD

Unveiling the Truth of Catholicism with
C. S. Lewis's *Mere Christianity*

Andrew Swafford

Ave Maria Press Notre Dame, Indiana

Scripture quotations are from the *Revised Standard Version of the Bible—Second Catholic Edition (Ignatius Edition)*, copyright © 2006 National Council of the Churches of Christ in the United States of America. Used by permission. All rights reserved.

Historical Evidence for New Testament Figures Table originally published in Lawrence Mykytiuk, "30 People in the New Testament Confirmed," *Bible History Daily* (blog), September 7, 2017. Used by permission.

© 2025 by Andrew Swafford

All rights reserved. No part of this book may be used or reproduced in any manner whatsoever, except in the case of reprints in the context of reviews, without written permission from Ave Maria Press®, Inc., P.O. Box 428, Notre Dame, IN 46556, 1-800-282-1865.

Founded in 1865, Ave Maria Press is a ministry of the United States Province of Holy Cross.

www.avemariapress.com

Paperback: ISBN-13 978-1-64680-407-8

E-book: ISBN-13 978-1-64680-408-5

Cover image © Getty Images.

Cover and text design by Andy Wagoner.

Printed and bound in the United States of America.

Library of Congress Cataloging-in-Publication Data is available.

TO MY WIFE, SARAH,
AND OUR SIX CHILDREN:
*Thomas, Fulton, Cate, Kolbe,
John Paul, and Avila*

Contents

Introduction ... ix

Part I: Who God Is and Who We Are

1. What Is a Human? and Why the Question of Humanity Matters ... 2
2. The Fulfillment of All Desire ... 8
3. I Want to Be Happy—So Why Should I Care About Morality? ... 15
4. Freedom and Virtue ... 21
5. What Are the Virtues? ... 28

Part II: On Jesus and His Divinity

6. Who Is Jesus, and How Can We Be Sure? ... 38
7. The Divinity of Jesus ... 51
8. The Resurrection of Jesus ... 60

Part III: The Jesus Effect

9. Did Jesus Found a Church? ... 69
10. The Difference Jesus Makes ... 80
11. Growing in the Spiritual Life: Chastity, Forgiveness, and Faith ... 92
12. *Mere* Catholicism: From the Trinity to the Eucharist—and Martyrdom ... 100

13. Does Christianity Really Work?	109
Acknowledgments	113
Historical Evidence for New Testament Figures Table by Lawrence Mykytiuk	115
Notes	124

Introduction

Who was C. S. Lewis, and what kind of book is *Mere Christianity*?

C. S. Lewis (1898–1963) was one of the foremost Christian thinkers of the twentieth century, and his thought remains lively and even timeless today, especially his classic work, *Mere Christianity*. Celebrated for its powerful and rational case for the Christian faith, this book was originally delivered as a series of legendary broadcast talks during World War II, and it continues to guide intellectual seekers toward a Christian understanding of morality, human nature, marriage, sin, forgiveness, faith, hope, and more. Lewis has the unique skill of being both profound and concise. For this reason, many come away from his works with a deeper conviction regarding the fundamentals of Christian faith and life. Indeed, his ability to make a reasoned case for the core of Christian faith is precisely his hallmark.

Many considering a conversion to Christ come away from Lewis with newfound zeal and confidence, and a fuller appreciation of the truth underpinning their turn toward Christ. This was exactly my experience when I first encountered *Mere Christianity* as a college student many years ago. Although I grew up Catholic, I never took my faith seriously until I had a deep conversion in college. Among other things, I had never encountered a confident and convincing explanation for the Christian faith. I found Lewis to be a rationally engaging, winsome, and joy-filled teacher. I came away with a strong sense that Christian faith was not something to be ashamed of or embarrassed about, but something to be proud of in the best sense. Lewis helped me to see who I was in Christ, and my life was never the same.

How did I come to Lewis, and what is the purpose of this book?

Because key teachers like Lewis (and Dr. Edward Sri, who was my undergraduate mentor) had such a large impact on me, I decided to devote my life to teaching theology, as a way to give back in the way they gave to me. Having now taught theology at Benedictine College for almost twenty years (and having taught two of Dr. Sri's children and one son-in-law), I have found it a tremendous joy to share Lewis's thought with the next generation, as I regularly use *Mere Christianity* (and his other works) in my classes. I have found that Lewis consistently touches every type of student—those who care deeply about their faith, as well as those who don't. His ability to get to the crux of an issue philosophically, with an eye toward its spiritual and existential payoff, is consistently illuminating and even life-changing. This is all very fitting, since the first time I heard Lewis's name was when Dr. Sri casually recommended *Mere Christianity* in class, when I was an undergraduate student at Benedictine College many years ago.

While Lewis is beloved by Christians of every stripe, this book will help you place his insights in a fuller Catholic context. As such, non-Catholic readers will receive the "merely Christian" approach, so beloved in Lewis's thought. But they will also be invited into a deeper next step, for to be Catholic is simply to be Christian with nothing left out. "Catholic," in fact, means "fullness" (or universal), as in fullness of faith, truth, and communion with God (see *CCC* 830).[1] So often, those who do convert from various branches of Christianity to the Catholic faith don't feel like they've left anything behind—rather, they feel as though they've embraced a fuller version of what they have always believed. This is what it means to come into "full" communion with Christ and his Church.

How should I read this book?

So, is this book about Lewis? Yes and no. Lewis is always in the background, and much of the book seeks to make accessible his insights regarding the truth of Christian faith and life. But there are also places where we seek to buttress Lewis's analysis. While *Mere Christianity* is a masterpiece, it says nothing about the Resurrection, or anything in defense of the historical Jesus, like whether or not we can truly trust the gospels and their witness to what Jesus said and did (spoiler: we can). Beefing up this background is essential for shoring up, for example, one of Lewis's most treasured arguments: that Jesus must be Lord, liar, or lunatic (that he cannot be merely a good man).

While our work will remain in close contact with Lewis's masterpiece, we do not presume that you are familiar with *Mere Christianity*, nor is there any need to have a copy of *Mere Christianity* close at hand.

You might think of our work as "Mere Christianity Plus." That is, we aim to do exactly what Lewis did more than half a century ago, but in an updated fashion, with some important and nuanced additions. One of these additions (apart from the historical trustworthiness of the gospels and Jesus's Resurrection) is to engage the question of whether Jesus founded a Church—whether he anticipated anything like an "organized religion." Lewis, himself, was a practicing Anglican and never shared anti-Catholic sentiment, so he wouldn't be far from our presentation here. In fact, although Lewis never became Catholic, his brother Warren nearly did so in the 1950s.[2] Still, over the years I have found that many non-Catholic readers of *Mere Christianity* gravitate toward a "nondenominational" ethos, making them somewhat averse to the importance of ecclesial doctrine (e.g., ancient creeds, church councils) and especially the sacraments.[3] In our treatment, we will seek to illumine how Catholicism provides a firmer grasp of the historical Jesus (seeing how the gospels are carried to us through Sacred Tradition), and we will also see how the story of salvation history finds its organic fulfillment in the Eucharistic liturgy of the Church. Accordingly, there will be stretches where we stay close to Lewis's thought and others where we ponder questions underlying his analysis.

Chapters 1–5 (Part I: Who God Is and Who We Are) examine questions foundational to the Christian life, drawing heavily from Lewis, such as *What does it mean to be human?*, *Does God exist?*, and *What is the moral life all about?* Here, with the help of Lewis, we explore the connection between virtue and human happiness. Chapters 6–8 (Part II: On Jesus and His Divinity) discuss the historical trustworthiness of the gospels, Jesus's divinity, and his Resurrection.

Chapters 9–13 (Part III: The Jesus Effect) show the link between Jesus and his ongoing ripple effects throughout history, starting with his founding of the Church and the importance of the Eucharist (chapter 9), as well as the existential difference he makes in our lives today when it comes to things like forgiveness, despair, and chastity (chapters 10 and 11). Chapter 12 draws from Lewis's insights about the heart of Christianity, so often lost on modern man: *Is Christianity just a nice moral program for society, or is it a participation in divine life?* Here, we see especially how Catholicism drives Lewis's analysis deeper and brings his treatment to completion in the Catholic faith. Chapter 13 concludes our journey, asking the existential question *Does Christianity work? Does Christian and in particular Catholic faith make a real difference in our lives?*

What should I expect to come away with?

Our goal is the same as that of Lewis in *Mere Christianity*: to make the case for Christian conviction (and to see its flowering in the Catholic faith). In short, the overarching goal of this book is to articulate why someone should be Catholic. But it does so by taking up Lewis's mantra, examining what it means to be "merely" Christian, as in getting to the very heart of the Christian faith. As mentioned earlier, this book is a sort of "Mere Christianity Plus," updating Lewis's already excellent treatment and showing how it organically flows into the Catholic fullness of faith.

We aim also to show the tremendous difference Christian faith makes in our lives. Apart from the very strong reasons historically and philosophically to believe in God, Jesus's divinity, and ultimately the Catholic Church, *Christian faith works*. That is, Christian faith bears immense fruit, especially at the human level of emotional and psychological wholeness, as well as marriage and family life—producing unrivaled peace, joy, meaning, and purpose in our lives, an aspect of Lewis's thought that is a balm to our modern age of isolation and aimlessness. And yet, despite the obvious reasons in its favor, faith can still seem scary, even terrifying. Christian faith can make perfect sense, and we can still find ourselves hesitating to commit our life to Christ. This is a telling fact concerning our task at hand, and quite significant for our own personal journey.

St. Augustine (354–430), during his tortuous journey away from and back to the Catholic faith, at one point described his perception that the "Catholic side [was] unbeaten but still not victorious."[4] His objections had been answered, but he was not ready to return and embrace the faith of his youth just yet. So also in our work here, we aim to remove objections and provide powerful reasons in support of Christian faith; but with Augustine, we recognize that this alone is not enough to "force one's hand," as it were.

In addition to the mystery of grace in the drama of conversion (surely at work in the life of Augustine), what generally brings someone to faith (in addition to hearing the reasons in defense of faith) is often twofold: religious experience (having a genuine encounter with the divine), and seeing the natural fruit of faith in people's lives. For this reason, we aim to illumine the human fruit that Christian faith yields. Indeed, we pray the reader comes away with a deep sense that Christian faith enables one to live a fuller human life—that Christian faith resonates deeply with the core of human experience. Once we see this, and with reasons in support of faith given, we will find there is nothing to lose and everything to gain by giving our lives entirely over to Jesus—making Christian faith eminently reasonable. Indeed, in the grand scheme of things, when all facets have been considered, perhaps we can even say it's unreasonable *not* to be a Christian. And yet in the drama of conversion—no matter how strong the evidence—there is always something beyond reason, entailing a personal entrustment to the one who reveals himself and seeks us out.

To use a personal example, when I married my wife twenty years ago, I didn't know who she would be decades into the future (though I had strong reasons to believe). I could never have discovered the joy of marriage had I not been willing to take the risk of entrusting my life to another. Saying yes to Christ is no different. This is the nature of life when it comes to what matters most. If we wait for absolute certainty, life will pass us by. For not to decide is to decide. More than just reason, we need courage and trust to open ourselves to this personal encounter with Christ. The joy of faith comes only on the heels of sincerely taking a chance on our Beloved—taking the risk of faith.

This book invites you to take a chance on Jesus and to see why that decision makes sense. It is indeed a risk, and potentially a frightening one at that. But there is much to gain, and very little (if anything) to lose in this glorious venture. So, what are we waiting for?

Part I
WHO GOD IS AND WHO WE ARE

ONE

What Is a Human? and Why the Question of Humanity Matters

What is a human being? What does it mean to be a person? Some might say humans are just the latest development in cosmic evolution, but that only speaks to humanity's physical traits. If we're merely physical beings, what does that mean for our dignity and the meaning of our lives? Is there such a thing as meaning that we did not create ourselves? Pondering these questions, we find ourselves asking, *Where did we come from? Who are we?* And *where are we going?*

The fact is, questions about the human person and the ultimate meaning of the cosmos—whether coming from the hand of a Creator, or simply the result of blind chance—are very much intertwined. When we reduce ourselves to being only physical, our value is understood simply in physical terms—how productive we can be and how useful we are to society. Equally disheartening is how we also lose all sense of trajectory and purpose, rendering our existence as an unintended product of physical forces.

But if we have a spiritual (nonmaterial) component, we can't *just* be the product of merely materialistic forces. And if there is a spiritual dimension within man, then the ultimate explanation of the universe can't *just* be matter—there must be more to us than molecules in motion. Indeed, the truth about humanity's nature points to the truth about the ultimate origin of all things. As humanity goes, so goes the question of God—and conversely, without the Creator, the creature vanishes.[1]

For these reasons, reflecting on the nature of the human person can be a privileged way into these ultimate questions. Our basic human experience can illumine the extraordinary implications lying on the other side of the ordinary, something that is at the heart of good philosophy.

C. S. Lewis and the Human Experience

So, what does it mean to be a person? Are we really different from the higher animals? And what about advanced machines and the wonders of artificial intelligence? One conclusion C. S. Lewis draws from our basic experience is that a human being is necessarily a *moral agent*—to be human is to have an inescapable sense of the moral order. As he observes, we uniquely "quarrel," whereas animals *fight*.[2] We quarrel because we believe that reason has something to say about moral matters, that moral disagreement isn't just a matter of personal preference and assertion of will.

While it might feel like morality is completely relative and everyone operates according to their own "truth," deep down we know morality is different from, say, a preference for certain flavors of ice cream. After all, we don't really argue about ice cream flavors, save in jest. And that's because we know that one's choice here is a matter of personal preference. But we *argue* about moral matters all the time—because we know there's a difference; the very presence of moral argument actually implies we believe morality is something objective and knowable.

If you doubt this, ask yourself how your day would go if you were to make a point of littering, parking in handicap spots (as a perfectly able person), or spouting off racial (or ableist) slurs. You would quickly find that people aren't as relativistic as they sometimes claim. They believe in an objective moral order, as humans always have—it's just that their priorities may have changed.

In the midst of moral argument, as Lewis notes, we don't appeal to force. We appeal to a *standard*. Consider remarks like these: "How'd you like it if someone did the same to you?" or "That's my seat; I was there first" or "Come on, you promised."[3] These remarks indicate more than that another's actions are not pleasing to us, or that their tastes happen to be different than ours. Rather, they imply that some objective *law* has been violated. Lewis writes:

> What interests me about all these remarks is that the man who makes them is not merely saying that the other man's behavior does not happen to please him. He is appealing to some kind of standard of behavior which he expects the other man to know about. And the other man very seldom replies: "To hell with your standard." Nearly always he tries to make out that what he has been doing does not really go against the standard, or that if it does there is some special excuse.[4]

We quarrel about moral matters (or make excuses and rationalizations) for the same reason we argue about referees in sports: because all sides begin with a shared understanding of the objective rules—and each side argues by showing that their actions are in accordance with the given rules. And "there would be no sense in trying to do that unless you and he *had some sort of agreement* as to what Right and Wrong are."[5]

But where did this moral standard come from? And what does our unique moral agency imply about our nature, and what does it say about the origin of the universe as a whole?

The Human Difference

While animals do amazing things, we partake in distinctive activities that demonstrate human uniqueness. These distinctive activities point to the distinctive (spiritual) capacity within our human nature, making us different in *kind*—not just degree—from the higher animals, because of our spiritual soul. For example:

We *make laws*.

We *recount history*.

We engage in *philosophy* and *science*, both of which entail an ability to distinguish between *appearance* and *reality*. As I've posed to my students, "Consider the stars of the night sky: Are they still up there?" They usually look at me with a bemused smirk. But then I explain that those stars are millions of light years away—and it takes a long time for that light to get to us. Isn't it possible that those stars could have exploded by now? This is a question only we ask—precisely because we can distinguish between *appearance* (the light in the night sky) and *reality* (the possibility that the star could have exploded by now).[6] A great deal of scientific and philosophical (and religious) thinking is based on this very distinction—between the way things appear and how they really are.

The *diversity of human dwellings* (in contrast to animal dwellings) reveals the presence of human reason and free will. A wren, for example, builds its nest according to its species, year after year. But consider the vast variety of human dwellings now and throughout time. The unique capacity of our nature is precisely what does not determine us in the same way as the animal kingdom, on account of human reason and human freedom.

We engage in *fine arts*—such as the Sistine Chapel. Such endeavors have no obvious utility, other than raising our minds and hearts to the transcendent.

We are uniquely *religious*, because we ask the ultimate questions and seek to honor and worship the most transcendent cause of all.

We *mass-produce tools*. While other animals have been known to use primitive tools, the mass production of tools by humans indicates our ability to separate the *idea* of a thing (its form or structure) from its individual (material) instantiation.[7]

We use *syntactical language*. Although other animals certainly communicate, they don't use similes and metaphors; they don't use prepositions and participles in complex ways. (After all, consider how many different ways we can use the word "in"—the dog is *in* the cage; sodium is *in* salt; the idea of a side is *in* a triangle; the idea is *in* my mind; love for my country is *in* my heart. Or consider how "before" can be used with reference to either space or time.)

Further, animals don't *translate* from one language to another. Consider where the meaning of a sentence is located, say, in an English sentence, alongside its German equivalent: Is there anything in the ink that equates the two? Certainly not. Rather, the equivalence lies in the *meaning* of one set of squiggly marks and the *meaning* of another set of squiggly marks—the meaning is *in one's mind*, not the ink![8]

Again, while animals certainly communicate and some have even been trained to mimic human language, you won't find animals discussing things like "the day after tomorrow."[9] When animals communicate (or even mimic human language), they are generally referring to some object of perception—something that can be sensed. That is, they don't refer to things that are not objects of sense perception, and certainly not to things that can't be sensed in principle—such as black holes, angels, or abstract numbers or mathematical concepts.

Herein, we can see that the uniqueness of human language flows from the uniqueness of human *reason*. The Greek word *logos* bears this out—a word that can mean "word" or "reason." We can utilize the power of *logos* ("word") because we are creatures who share in *logos* (reason), all of which is rooted in the Eternal Logos, the Word of God made flesh (see John 1:1–4, 14).

And finally, as moral and rational agents, we are *responsible* in an utterly unique way. While animals may act for reasons and purposes, only we ask the higher-order question: Are the reasons for which we are acting truly *good* reasons? This brings us to the unique human threshold of conscience and morality.[10] The animal world acts based on instinct; we act for reasons—and can reflect upon those reasons with an awareness not present in the animal kingdom. All of this manifests the unique spiritual powers of human intellect and will.

Artificial Intelligence

While the above items point out the essential difference between man and animals, you might be wondering, "Sure, but what about machines—*what about AI?*" Certainly, artificial intelligence continues to impress us day after day, and it poses vexing problems for academic honesty and integrity.

Traditionally, one would point out that a computer is no more "aware" of its knowledge than a library is aware of the contents of its books.[11] Or, as Mortimer Adler argued at the turn of the last century, artificial intelligence can be said to match the human mind when a computer is able to have a long "conversation."[12] However, in recent years, we have seen artificial intelligence approximate (and in certain ways, greatly surpass) human intelligence, calling for further reflection on our part.

While a long-standing tradition seeks to define man as a "rational animal," going back to the likes of Aristotle,[13] the consideration of AI forces us to go beyond our mere rational capacities to identify our distinctive difference, over against machines. As an embodied person, man straddles the material and spiritual spheres of reality. This connects us both to the intellectual realm of angels (and in some ways, the rational realm of artificial intelligence) and to the bodily and emotional realm of the animal kingdom.

While the unique human capacities above point to our rational dimension (over against the animal kingdom), what seems to most distinctively separate us from the wonders of artificial intelligence is that we *care*. In the words of John Haugeland, "The trouble with artificial intelligence is that computers *don't give a damn*."[14]

The *anxiety* about the human project (the fear that my life is worthless, the angst over whether my motives are truly authentic or whether I am motivated by fear of others' disapproval) is at the heart of the human quest. To be human is to ask these deep (and sometimes dark) questions. To be human is to take *responsibility* for our answers to these questions. As my friend and colleague James Madden puts it: "Can a computer put itself into question? Can it face the grave consequences of seeing its way of life as a failure? Could machines *question their own motives* for running their programs?"[15]

We ask the hard questions because we care. We read and write books like this because we care. This existential care separates us from machines (and animals), making us uniquely *embodied persons*—with a spiritual component that is rational and free, yet embodied and full of emotion and angst.

We can see this existential "care" as a call to responsibility, ultimately from our Creator to live a reflective and meaningful life—to take seriously the cues he has left us regarding our fundamental meaning and purpose. This existential care points to our primordial human vocation:

We are made to *wonder*.
We are made for moral *responsibility*.
We are made for *meaning* and *purpose*.

Our wonder, responsibility, and the ultimate meaning and purpose of our lives are found in God, the Creator of all things. Without him, we eventually lose our grip on our true and definitive story.

Over the next four chapters, we will more robustly survey reasons to believe in God and what human life is all about. Much of our discussion that follows is inspired by Aristotle and the virtue tradition, which Lewis unpacks so well. After developing a deep picture of what human flourishing looks like, we will turn to Jesus—why we can trust the gospels and his Resurrection. Our task is to give a reason for the hope that lies within (see 1 Peter 3:15).

TWO
The Fulfillment of All Desire

So, how do we come to recognize the hand of God? Is there a rational ladder upon which we can make our assent? The *Catechism of the Catholic Church* (*CCC*) speaks of two general ways of coming to God: from the *world* and from the *person* (see 32–33). Our discussion here is a precursor to faith, providing the rational foundations that enable us to receive the Gospel of Jesus Christ.

From the World

Contingency

Traditional arguments from the world refer to things like the contingency and fundamental order of the cosmos. If something is "contingent," it is *dependent* and doesn't explain itself. To say the universe is contingent is simply to say *it doesn't explain where everything came from*. More strictly, something is contingent if (1) it doesn't have to be the way it is and (2) it doesn't *have* to be here at all.

The changes present in the universe (in big and small ways) are clear signs of its contingency. For example, in the traditional account of the Big Bang (which was established by a Catholic priest named Fr. Georges Lemaître), the universe (along with space and time) *began* in the finite past (some 13.8 billion years ago).[1] In our experience, what begins has a cause—what begins is necessarily contingent.

Generally, the philosophical tradition rooted in Plato, Aristotle, St. Augustine, and St. Thomas Aquinas sees the following traits as clear signs of contingency:

- Being able to *change*
- Being *physical* or *material*
- Being *temporal* (bound by time)
- Being able to *be different than the way it is* (that is, if something could have been otherwise than it is)[2]

Here is the important point: Whatever falls into this category (i.e., contingent beings) is *caused* by something else. That is, contingent beings don't explain themselves but point beyond themselves to their ultimate explanation. Such contingent, dependent factors can't go on to infinity—because then nothing would ultimately be explained. You might think of it this way: *Zero times infinity is still zero.* Everything can't be a *dependent* being; otherwise, nothing would exist—*for from nothing, nothing comes.*

Here's an image that captures this dynamic. Suppose you see a chain hanging in the sky, and you ask me why it's hanging there, and I respond, "There are an *infinite number of chain links going upward.*" You would look at me and say, "Uh, okay, but that doesn't explain why there is a chain hanging in the sky."

But suppose I answer by explaining that—even though we can't see it—the chain is actually *hanging from a skyscraper* way up in the sky. This would be an explanation. The skyscraper explains its own standing; and the chain is hanging because it is dependent upon the skyscraper.[3] In this analogy, the skyscraper stands for God (who is the source of his own existence), and the chain stands for all created things (whose existence is always fundamentally contingent and dependent).

Logically, contingency must lead back to necessity. So, all accounts must come back to something that is *necessary*, that explains itself. For the atheist, this is the universe and its fundamental laws. But in the words of Catholic physicist Stephen Barr, the "psychology" of the atheist is to take things *for granted*—here, the universe and its fundamental order.[4] The theist continues to ask *why*—why is the universe the way it is, and why does anything exist at all, rather than nothing?

Order and Design

The design present in the universe—especially in things that lack intelligence—implies an intelligence outside the universe, the divine mind as the cause of all things. To use the image associated with William Paley (1743–1805), if we found a watch along the shores of a beach, we wouldn't hesitate to assume that someone with intelligence made and designed the watch. If we say that about a watch, how much more so the complexity of the cosmos—from the molecular cell to distant galaxies? Today, however, the reader is probably thinking, "*Yes, but what about evolution?*"[5] For this reason, it's important to go deeper in terms of what we mean by design.

At a fundamental level, on the assumption of atheism, should we expect a law-like, mathematically rational universe, such as we have? After all, why should nonthinking matter function according to mathematical laws? Is this a given that can be taken for granted? As with the above, the theist continues to ask *why*—why is the universe the way it is, why is it law governed at all?

Against the Christian backdrop of an all-wise Creator, the rationality embedded in the universe (making disciplines like physics and chemistry possible) makes perfect sense. And if we are created in his image and likeness, it makes sense that we can (at least partially) understand this fundamental order. This is the perspective that convinced long-time atheist Antony Flew:

> If you accept the fact that there are laws, then something must impose that regularity on the universe. . . . Those scientists who point to the Mind of God do not merely advance a series of arguments or a process of syllogistic reasoning. Rather, they propound a vision of reality that emerges from the conceptual heart of modern science and imposes itself on the rational mind. It is a vision that I personally find compelling and irrefutable.[6]

For the Christian, it's fitting that creation participates in the rationality of the Creator because it was *thought* into existence by the divine mind—just as the blueprint of a building first exists in the mind of an architect and is only later embodied in brick and mortar.[7] Even in our sciences, then, we are retracing God's thoughts after him (see *CCC* 159). In this way, we can see design in the most fundamental order of the cosmos (in addition to various biological systems).[8] After all, scientists don't invent but *discover* the laws of nature. There must be a *rational order embedded in reality* to make science possible in the first place, which is exactly what Flew's comments above are getting at.

This is what Pope Benedict XVI had in mind when he said that science raises a question that "points beyond itself."[9] Science is possible because *Mind precedes matter*; that's why reality is brimming with *Logos* (reason)—because it's the embodiment of a divine idea.[10]

From the Person

What is closer to home for us, as we saw in the last chapter, is the fundamental structure of the human person. As the *Catechism* states:

With his openness to truth and beauty, his sense of moral goodness, his freedom and the voice of his conscience, with his longings for the infinite and for happiness, man questions himself about God's existence. In all this he discerns signs of his spiritual soul. *The soul, the "seed of eternity we bear in ourselves, irreducible to the merely material" [GS 18], can have its origin only in God.* (33, emphasis added)

Can this world be all there is—when everything within us clamors for more? Either life is absurd, in that we have an ache for eternity, for which no fulfillment is possible (as some atheist existentialist philosophers have claimed),[11] or these yearnings are a sign of our ultimate homeland, not in this life but the next.

So, how do we "read" the human condition? What does it all mean?

Human Desire

C. S. Lewis describes three competing interpretations of this human angst: the *Fool's Way*, the *Way of the Disillusioned "Sensible Man,"* and the *Christian Way*.[12]

The *Fool's Way* places the blame for our unhappiness and lack of fulfillment on external circumstances—just bad luck. The fool "goes on all his life thinking that if only he tried *another woman*, or went for a *more expensive holiday*, or whatever it is, then, *this time*, he really would catch the mysterious something we are all after."[13] A great many people simply float through life this way, aimlessly wandering from one thing (or relationship) to the next.

The *Disillusioned "Sensible Man"* realizes the folly of the fool's way, but his response is fundamentally jaded. Believing that human happiness can't be found, he decides *it's best not to hope for such fulfillment* and to just accept our fate. Again, how many folks—especially as the enthusiasm of youth wanes and life turns out differently than expected—find themselves in this predicament? Many at this point have simply given up on the prospect of joy. To their credit, Lewis acknowledges, this "would be the best line we could take if man did not live forever."[14]

But what if there's more?

On the *Christian* reading, we were never meant to find our definitive beatitude here, so we shouldn't be surprised that even the best of earthly lives still leaves us yearning for more. This does not mean that this fundamental ache in the human heart is meaningless. Rather, it's a sign of our ultimate destiny.

Other innate desires, arising from within our nature, such as thirst, hunger, and the sex appetite, point to real objects that fulfill those desires.[15] For this reason, Lewis concludes, "If I find in myself a desire which no experience in this world can satisfy, *the most probable explanation is that I was made for another world.*"[16] What emerges for Lewis is a sacramental view of creation and human desire—as truly good, but pointing beyond itself:

> I must take care, on the one hand, never to despise, or be unthankful for these earthly blessings, and on the other, never to mistake them for the something else of which they are only a kind of *copy* or *echo*, or *mirage*. I must keep alive in myself the desire for my true country, which I shall not find till after death; I must never let it get snowed under or turned aside; I must make it the main object of life to press on to that other country and to help others to do the same.[17]

Our Lord calls us to hunger and thirst for righteousness (Mt 5:6)—do we see our physical hunger as a sign of this deeper hunger within us? In the words of St. Augustine, "[You] made us and draw us to yourself, and our heart is unquiet until it rests in you."[18] Our restless hearts pine for many things, but behind the veil of the "many" is a thirst for the *One*.

What Does the Voice of Conscience Mean?

The voice of conscience is not only a window into our deepest self, but also the echo of God's voice within,[19] the "still small voice" (1 Kgs 19:12) of the one who knows us by name and calls us to an end beyond time (see Isaiah 43:1). This is why Lewis writes, "You find out more about God from the moral law than from the universe in general, just as you find out more about a man by listening to his conversation than by looking at a house he has built."[20]

The moral law, in Lewis's words, "is hard as nails."[21] He says this because we know, as we saw in the last chapter, that *right is right*, and *wrong is wrong*. This is why we so ardently make excuses or rationalizations—because we desperately want to justify ourselves; we know we are *responsible* to this most solemn of voices, this most solemn of truths.

We really can't bear it otherwise. And this is exactly where Lewis wants to bring us: to the recognition that we have come up short, that our excuses are just that—*excuses*. The danger at this stage is the worship of the self, the desire to be our own absolute. We know we are *responsible*, but to whom? Indeed, there is a great temptation to "be our own boss." But consider times when your reason and passions were at odds. In those moments, you have two options: you can conform your passions to right reason; or you can cook up some good reasons to justify doing what you want to do. The latter so often marks the human condition.

St. John Henry Newman once said that the elevation of "private judgment" is the first principle of Protestantism.[22] One can see this principle transposed into the modern world in the supreme elevation of private judgment, with each of us claiming sovereignty over not only what is true and false, but even over the reality of our own bodies, sex, gender, and so on.[23]

Accepting conscience as the voice of God is the recognition that *someone is above me*. I am responsible to Another.

So, why believe in a Creator?

Because it makes the most sense of our experience.[24]

This becomes all the more apparent when we acknowledge the abject failure of reducing reality merely to the quantifiable and measurable. While the scientific method is very good at capturing this aspect of reality, the move from "that which is accessible to the scientific method" to "that which is accessible to the scientific method *is equal to all that exists*" is a *philosophical* claim, not a scientific one.[25]

Even those who claim to hold such a philosophical worldview seldom *live* by that worldview. After all, does anyone really believe their love for their spouse or children is merely a matter of molecules in motion? Does anyone really believe that there is no moral fact of the matter—that all moral claims are equal to one another, and that there has been no moral progress? How would anyone actually go about living in accordance with such ideas—is that even possible?

To see the stark alternative, consider the following comments from a contemporary atheist, Alex Rosenberg:

> We have to acknowledge (to ourselves, at least) that many questions we want the "right" answers to just don't have any. These are questions about the morality of stem-cell research or abortion or affirmative action or gay marriage or our obligations to future generations. Many enlightened people, including many scientists, think that reasonable people can eventually find the right answers to such questions. *Alas, it will turn out that all anyone can really find are the answers they like.* The

same goes for those who disagree with them. Real moral disputes can be ended in lots of ways: by voting, by decree, by fatigue of the disputants, by the force of example that changes social mores. *But they can never really be resolved by finding the correct answers. There are none.*[26]

However, if there has been moral progress, as people almost universally assume, that means we have come closer to the moral truth on certain matters (e.g., equal human dignity, regardless of race). And yet moral truths don't fit in a test tube—they can't be measured or quantified. So, either moral truths are a matter of mere preference (like one's choice of ice cream flavors, as Rosenberg articulates above)—a view very few outside of academic circles would affirm—or pretending that reality can be reduced to the merely quantifiable and measurable is false.

All of our experience (all of the evidence) points to the latter: Reality is more expansive than merely what fits in the scientific method—reality is bigger than what can be quantified and measured. Therefore, to be fully rational, we must take into account *all* of the data—not just what fits into the scientific method. To do otherwise not only loses our grip on our humanity, but forfeits our grasp on an important dimension of reality—in fact, we lose our grip on the most important aspects of the real.

This material world is changing and fleeting because it is ultimately contingent and points beyond itself. The order that we see is the embodiment of divine wisdom—from the farthest galaxy to the incredible language of our genetic code. The spiritual capacities latent within human nature, our desire for infinite happiness, and the voice of conscience (and the moral law within) all point beyond the material order. They are only really accounted for by the supposition that God is the source of all that is.

Lack of meaning and purpose brings about debilitating depression and loneliness, far more than mere low self-esteem. As then-Cardinal Ratzinger put it, *meaning that is self-made is no meaning at all.*[27] What we long for is meaning that's *received*. True received meaning comes from the hand of our Creator, who is the source of our moral experience and the ultimate object of our desire. He is the one who has made us for "a time such as this" (Est 4:14), casting each of us in a pivotal role for the unique time given to us.

The Christian reading of the human condition is that life is not absurd. It makes sense because God is the ground of all existence and the source of the moral law within. Indeed, he is the ultimate goal and fulfillment of every human desire.

THREE

I Want to Be Happy— So Why Should I Care About Morality?

One of the great apologias of the Christian life is the appeal of this way of life, when it is lived out in a healthy and constructive way—when we allow the Christian way of life to penetrate the human dimension so that the supernatural order of grace transforms us from within.

While Jesus most fully reveals God to us, *he also reveals us to ourselves.*[1] This is Christian humanism: *Jesus teaches us most fully what it means to be human*; and conversely, all that is authentically human can be rightly taken up into the Gospel. Herein, we see that Christian faith does not alienate—does not make us less human—but rather enables us to live the fully human life. In this light, the *human* fruit of the Christian life is a perennial sign of its supernatural truth.

Law—Friend or Foe to Freedom and Flourishing?

So often today we think of morality as *restrictive*, as rules imposed from above that keep us from doing what we want—arbitrary dictates that take away our "fun." Against this backdrop and capturing a much more profound outlook, Lewis opens his moral section in *Mere Christianity* with this observation: "Moral rules are directions for running the human machine."[2]

Although we're accustomed to think of morality as stipulations or rules imposed by a higher authority that infringe upon our freedom, classical Christian thinkers see things in a different light. Throughout the Bible and Catholic tradition, there is a strong sense that the law (especially the moral law) is actually a *friend to freedom*, not its enemy (see Psalm 119). Why would the ancients see it this way? From this perspective, morality is fundamentally not about "rules" but about human *flourishing*, that is, *happiness* in a deep and objective sense.

Our human nature is latent with various powers and capacities (to think, love, and feel). We are made to know and contemplate the truth and love the good—and to love the good not in a disembodied way but *viscerally*, with our whole being (including our emotions). Human nature begins in potency, with these various capacities and desires propelling us into life, yearning for the reality that fulfills our nature.

"Potency" is a concept derived from Aristotle and St. Thomas Aquinas referring to a thing's innate capacity to develop into the fullness of whatever kind of thing it is (e.g., an acorn becoming an oak tree). The potency of a thing is rooted in its particular nature, which inclines it toward its "end," the fully actualized form of itself. Thus, there's a gap between "human nature as is" and "human nature as fully actualized."[3] While this can be understood in terms of physical maturation,[4] it also applies to our spiritual and moral development, as we grow in our pursuit of virtue. The moral life is about going from point A to point B, from the potential powers of our human nature to fully actualizing those powers. For the likes of Aristotle, *happiness, then, is the full actualization of this potency, the fulfillment of our spiritual and moral capacities.* Herein lies the flourishing (or full actualization) of our human nature.

If we have such capacities and leave them dormant, we shouldn't be surprised to find ourselves unfulfilled, restless, and unhappy in the deepest of senses. Clearly, "happiness" here is not merely something that happens to us, as if it were nothing more than a subjective state of contentment. Rather, the entire moral life in the classical Catholic tradition is a journey toward authentic happiness, a journey toward genuine human fulfillment.

When Lewis describes morality as "rules for running the human machine," he means there is a fit between the moral law and human nature. Conversely, breaking the rules isn't just about the rules. It's about the corruption of the "machine," leading to its inability to run the way it was designed.

While there will be plenty of times when the "right" thing doesn't seem to lead to happiness, the Christian conviction is that it will in the end. Sometimes duty calls us to act contrary to our immediate self-interest; but when we do so, we are in the process of becoming the kind of people who can attain real and lasting happiness. By analogy, much training of an athlete runs contrary to one's initial inclination. But in the end, fulfilling such "duties" (say, in a training regimen) leads to the better flourishing of the athlete.

What Lewis is getting at above comes out when we compare the classical Catholic view of the moral life to what emerges in the fourteenth century and flowers in the centuries following (both in the Reformation and the Enlightenment) and is very much present in our consciousness today. This fourteenth-century development is tied up with a philosophical doctrine known as "nominalism" and is associated with William of Ockham.[5] This nominalist development is known as the *via moderna* ("modern way") and is set in contrast to the classical Catholic approach, known as the *via antiqua* ("ancient way").[6]

A warning to the reader: This next section can sound a bit abstract at first, but it has *huge* implications; understanding the changes taking place here goes a long way toward understanding the moral predicament in which we find ourselves today.

Briefly, nominalism is the view that natures of things aren't real. So, when we speak of a common "human nature" (or a common nature of anything, whether a cow, a lizard, or a carbon atom), our language doesn't correspond to anything real that these things share in common, making them what they are. For the nominalist, we use common words (or common nouns) like "dog" or "cow" as convenient shorthand. But these are just *names* (hence the term *nominalism*)—that is, these are mere *words*. Our language, for the nominalist, therefore, does not capture anything meaningful about reality.[7] Though abstract, nominalism has enormous implications. If there is no such thing as a shared human nature, then there can be no common (or objective) human morality—and no common pattern of human life that will universally bring about human flourishing.[8]

Another important position that tracks closely with nominalism is *voluntarism*. Voluntarism is a view of God that elevates his *will* above his intellect, as an attempt to accentuate the transcendence and supreme power of God. The question is classically posed in Plato's *Euthyphro* when Socrates asks if an action is *pious because the gods love it*, or if *the gods love an action because it's pious*.[9] To go with the former is to say that goodness is simply the result of an arbitrary decision of the gods (i.e., voluntarism). To opt for the latter is to point to something objective in the action that is *inherently* good, which explains why the gods approve it.

While trying to preserve God's transcendence, voluntarism leads to troubling implications—principally, the view that something is good *only because God wills it*, with the result that God could have willed its opposite. For the voluntarist, God could have commanded, "Thou shall commit adultery" and "Thou shall commit blasphemy," and such actions would thereby become good, simply because God said so.[10]

The question is truly a difficult one. In effect, one has three options: (a) God is not bound by reason or logic at all (i.e., voluntarism); (b) God worships another "god" called "logic" and is bound by its precepts; or (c) strange as it may sound, the laws of logic, truth, and reason are actually rooted in God's very nature—and God can't contradict himself (as not a defect, but a perfection).

The classical Christian answer is the third one. It's not that God lacks power, and it's not that he is beholden to something outside himself. But he is beholden to himself. He is the author of human nature (and all natures), which finds its source in a perfection that preexists in God himself.[11] The reason one can say that God *cannot* command adultery or blasphemy is that such actions are incompatible with the authentic flourishing of human nature—a human nature that is rooted in God himself (and God can't contradict himself).[12] So, there is something objective about the moral law—it's not arbitrary. Human nature has an objective content, rooted in God, which orients human flourishing within objective parameters—which is precisely why Lewis states that the moral law constitutes instructions for running the human machine.[13]

For now, let's contrast the salient aspects of the *via moderna* (informed by nominalism and voluntarism) and the *via antiqua* (the classical Catholic approach to the moral life).

Via Moderna	Via Antiqua
Human nature is not real (nominalism).	*Human nature is real* (there really is something we have in common that makes us true members of an ontological category—a common essence or nature that makes us human).

I Want to Be Happy—So Why Should I Care About Morality?

Moral law has no direct connection to human nature (because human nature is not real). The moral law is only *arbitrarily* connected to human nature and has no inherent connection to human flourishing or happiness.	Moral law is directly fitted to the flourishing of human nature (as "instructions for running the human machine"). The moral law constitutes instructions for human happiness.
The moral law is imposed arbitrarily from above and has no inherent connection to human nature and human happiness (voluntarism).	God's power is always guided by his wisdom (see *CCC* 271), which means that his giving of the moral law is never merely a "power play." Rather, his law flows out of his wisdom and is given for our good.
God is viewed more as Master than Father. If his law is not guided by his wisdom and is not inherently connected to our flourishing and beatitude, it feels like a constraint imposed upon us by way of power (not truth or love).	*God is a loving Father, not mere Master.* His commands are ordered to our good and flourishing—our happiness. The drama of the sin in the garden has a lot to do with the Evil One portraying God as an overbearing master whose law seeks to keep us back from something, some happiness he supposedly doesn't want us to have (see Genesis 3:1, 4, and *CCC* 397).[14]
Freedom is diminished by law. In this analysis, God is the most "free" because he can do whatever he wants. Our freedom is curtailed by the imposition of God's law. If we obey, we do so out of fear, not for our own good (because, again, the law has no inherent connection to our good or happiness).	*True freedom lies in our ability to do the good.*[15] Freedom is not mere choice but is ordered to growth in our ability to do the good. Freedom is ordered toward authentically loving the good. Accordingly, as we mature on the journey, the law becomes *a friend to freedom*—as we eventually internalize the law and obey it from within. We obey not out of fear but out of *love*—we come to love the good, to which the law beckons us.

At a deep level, in the classical Catholic view, we don't so much break the law *as the moral law breaks us*. That is, our defiance of the moral law doesn't lead to freedom, but to slavery. This is the path of addiction, the loss of freedom. In contrast, training in the moral order—under the tutelage of the moral law—leads to *self-mastery*, which makes possible *self-gift*. True freedom is not its own end but is ordered to love.[16]

Initially, we might feel the strain of the law—just as we might feel uncomfortable at the beginning of our coach's conditioning program. But over time, the law becomes internalized, and we get into better shape. The trained athlete gets to the point where they actually *want* to live out their coach's prescriptions. They *want* to train. This is what it means to *internalize* the law. This training is the precondition for love, for self-gift. Thus, the training of an athlete (or a musician) captures perfectly the journey of the moral life. For me, coming to grips with this concept changed everything. I knew what it meant to train in athletics. Translating this blood, sweat, and tears to the game of life gave me meaning and purpose beyond anything I could have imagined prior.

So, why care about training in the moral life? *Precisely because* we want to be truly happy, to flourish and live well. Deep down, we know that relationships are at the core of a meaningful life—our ability to love is at the center of a life filled with purpose. And to love well requires the freedom to rise above ourselves and make a sincere gift of ourselves, as Christ exemplifies on the Cross (see John 15:13).

Indeed, the pursuit of virtue—or training in the moral life—*gives us the freedom to love*.

FOUR
Freedom and Virtue

It's common today for people to think of morality along the following lines: "If I'm not hurting anyone, can't I just do what I want?" So often in the modern context we think in a minimalistic fashion. We want to know *at what point we have broken the rules*. Beyond that, we're often more or less unconcerned.[1] But could you imagine playing a sport that way—by just asking at what point you've "broken the rules"? That certainly wouldn't be a recipe for excellence, or even enjoying the sport.

We might also ask: How has this moral minimalist mentality fared? Do people today have a greater sense of purpose in their lives? Has it brought them a greater sense of mission in their pursuit of happiness? Or is it part and parcel of the dreariness of modern life, with people feeling adrift in their search for meaning, as they find themselves awash in a bastion of loneliness and isolation?

For many people today, *life is a story with no plot*. No longer is there any sense of *received* meaning or purpose, something *given*—by God, tradition, or nature (or all the above). We are forced to make our own meaning and find our own sense of purpose. And we feel deeply in our bones the hollowness of this endeavor: As we mentioned earlier, *meaning that is self-made is no meaning at all*. We long for meaning that is received, that has an objective anchor and calls us forth; we long to be cast in the divine drama, with each of us having a unique and important part to play.[2] So, how can we forge a deeper view of human life and flourishing?

A Fleet of Ships

Lewis proposes an analogy to capture the journey of the moral life—as a *fleet of ships*.[3] He offers three principles for this human voyage to go well:

- The ships *cannot collide* with one another.
- Each ship must be *seaworthy*.
- All the ships must be traveling *in the same direction*, toward a *common destination*.[4]

The first principle embraces the partial truth expressed in the modern sentiment above: We should avoid harming each other. The second principle points to the importance of virtue, particularly with reference to the training of our passions and desires. If a ship's motor or steering apparatus isn't working—no matter how good the intentions—*the broken-down ship will eventually hit another ship.*

Addictive behaviors offer an apt illustration here. Countless families have been racked with the consequences of mere "personal sins," which supposedly weren't "hurting anybody," like alcoholism, drugs, or a gambling addiction. The same is true of pornography. What begins as a "private sin" eventually reaps hugely destructive consequences, in our own lives and those around us. In this light, self-mastery is not only the precondition for true love—but also requisite to ensure we don't harm those around us.

Lewis's third principle concerns how our fundamental beliefs about the meaning and purpose of life influence how we go about this human journey. Do we see life as having a preordained and overarching goal, in which our individual endeavors and pursuits take shape? Or is nothing preordained—do we decide *everything*, including the ultimate end of our lives? As Lewis puts it: "Does it not make a great difference whether his ship is his own property or not? Does it not make a great difference whether I am, so to speak, the landlord of my own mind and body, or only a tenant, responsible to the real landlord?"[5]

What Is Man's End?

Classical philosophy (manifest, say, in Aristotle) and classical Christian faith see life as having a built-in purpose and meaning. We receive this meaning upon our entrance into the world, and this *received meaning* constitutes a call from the power that made us, beckoning us to our final end. It is rooted in human nature and points to the transcendent fulfillment of our nature.

The Greek word for end, purpose, or goal here is *telos*. For Aristotle, we reach this end by fully actualizing our human nature—by actualizing the powers and capacities latent within our nature. This process of actualization is precisely where we find happiness, authentic human flourishing.

This full actualization of our nature comes about through virtue, and ultimately through our coming to know and contemplate the highest truth and coming into union with the highest good. Though opaque, even Aristotle sees this journey as culminating in rational contact with the Uncaused Cause of all things.[6] Aristotle also sees a significant place for *friendship* in the well-lived human life, in which case there is a clear *relational* fulfillment of our human nature.[7]

In this light, especially as enhanced and elevated by the classical Christian tradition, we can propose the following as the meaning and purpose of human life, our human *telos* (Lewis's *common destination* above):

- *Happiness* (as the objective perfecting and flourishing of our nature)
- *Union with God* (we are made to know the most ultimate Truth and love the highest Good; our intellect and will won't come to rest until they rest in God himself)
- *Fulfillment of our relationships* (becoming a good son, daughter, husband, wife, father, mother, friend, teacher, doctor, craftsman, farmer, etc.)

Again, *growth in virtue is the means by which we attain our end* in this threefold manner. Through growth in virtue we move from human-nature-as-is (in potency) to human-nature-as-fully-actualized (true happiness). Through growth in virtue we journey back to God. And virtue constitutes the set of human skills required to fulfill our relationships—to be a *good* husband, wife, father, mother, friend, son, daughter, and so on. If I do not become virtuous, I won't be able to fulfill these fundamental relationships—I won't be able to be the husband or wife, father or mother I want to be.

For this reason, *virtues are the skills needed to live life with excellence*, to live a *good* human life—to become truly happy. Growth in virtue enables us to attain self-possession, self-mastery. And self-mastery is what enables us to make a gift of ourselves in love, to God and neighbor. Hence, the moral life is not simply about *my* life and doing what *I* want—that's actually a recipe for misery and unfulfillment.[8]

Modernity   *Classical Catholic View*

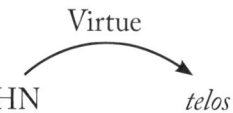

- happiness (as the full actualization of our nature)
- union with God
- fulfillment of our relationsips (communion through total self-gift)

While giving talks to young people over the years, my wife and I have asked audiences, "How many of you want to marry a selfish person?" No one's hand goes up. Sometimes we'll follow up, asking, "How many of you want *to be* the selfish person in a relationship?" Again, no hands go up. If no one wants this, then how does it happen (to varying degrees)?

We arrive in such a state in our relationships because we lack virtue—because bad habits have overtaken our lives, and we have lost some of our freedom, our freedom to love. We get there because we lack deep healing and have failed to find wholeness, our true center of gravity. In other words, virtue, wholeness, holiness, and genuine psychological and emotional health all go together. Virtue is about *integration*, putting the pieces of our life back together. It's about finding our true and abiding anchor and center of gravity, ultimately in Christ Jesus.

Vice and sin disrupt this unity and scatter us. In the words of St. Augustine, when he turned away from God and became enmeshed in sin, he "*went to pieces.*"[9] In turning away from God, *he lost himself.*

What Is True Freedom?

Freedom in the virtue tradition is greater than the absence of external constraint. More than just the license to do whatever we want whenever we want, true freedom is the *ability to do the good*.[10] The key to this freedom is that it can *grow* over time and with practice. We can quickly recognize this freedom by looking at a few familiar illustrations:

- Learning a foreign language
- Learning a musical instrument
- Acquiring an athletic skill
- Getting in shape

Each one of these examples displays a freedom that can grow over time with progress and training, as one becomes increasingly adept at a given practice or craft (or acquiring greater physical endurance). What begins as arduous or clumsy eventually becomes second nature, with time and discipline. Practice here makes—if not perfect, more and more *permanent*, as the given skill becomes more deeply ingrained within us.[11]

Aristotle points out that the pleasure or pain accompanying an action is an index of our character.[12] He doesn't mean that the pleasure or pain of an action is an indication of whether the action is good or evil. Rather, he means that the pleasure or pain *accompanying* an action is an indication of how far along we are in mastering that particular virtue. If I'm especially pained by a courageous act, that's a sign I still have a way to go before mastering this virtue. While some virtues will always entail a certain degree of pain in their performance (e.g., courage), the more seasoned and practiced I am, the easier the practice of those virtues will become (and the freer I become to perform such actions).

There's an important distinction between performing an *individual* virtuous act and possessing a particular virtue as an *ingrained habit*. It's one thing to hit a lucky shot—it's another thing to be a skilled player who is consistent and reliable. Similarly, it's one thing to act virtuously once; it's another thing to have developed a sustained pattern of acting—an ingrained disposition—to do the right thing, almost instinctively.

We like to think that we'll be heroes in the crisis situations we imagine for ourselves in the distant future. But what's more likely is that at those moments, our masks will come off. Our true selves—the ingrained habits we have developed for years—will come to light. In the words of Lewis:

> Surely what a man does when he is taken off his guard is the best evidence for what sort of a man he is? Surely what pops out before the man has time to put on a disguise is the truth? If there are rats in a cellar you are most likely to see them if you come in very suddenly. But the suddenness does not create the rats: it only prevents them from hiding.[13]

If we want to be the "hero" when it counts, we will have needed thousands of reps along the way. Just as with an athlete: Without years of preparation and practice, no one is going to shoot a basketball like Steph Curry. So, why would we think we can just flip a switch in the moral life when it becomes crucial—when the stakes are raised?[14]

When we fully develop a virtue (as an internal disposition that becomes part of us), we are able to perform the action:

- *Consistently*
- *Promptly*
- *With joy*

We get there by repeatedly performing this virtuous act. We become courageous people by performing courageous acts. The same is true with justice, temperance, or any other virtue.

Similar acts over time inculcate similar habits deep within us. They become part of us. This is how the law becomes *internalized*: What was hard in the beginning becomes second nature to us, to the point where we feel awkward doing it the "wrong" way—because the good habit has become so deeply ingrained within us. This dynamic is true of both virtue and vice, both for good and bad habits. Like acts become like habits. Over time, they become an essential part of *who* we are.

Who Do I Want to Be?

One of the most important things about the life of virtue is the *continuity* it shows in one's life. As mentioned above, we often think of the moral life as a set of discrete, *disconnected* moral dilemmas we'll face at various points in our life—big crisis moments, as it were. While these decision points are critically important, we often forget that what we will decide then *has virtually been decided* by the habits we have built up over time.

It is common today to radically distinguish *who we are* from *what we do*. And while there's some truth here (after all, we will make mistakes), this modern sentiment can easily go too far. After all, imagine if I said, "*Deep down, I'm a great pitcher—I just never throw strikes.*" That would be absurd.

Every pitch I throw with poor mechanics (and miss the strike zone) makes it more likely that I'll throw with poor mechanics the next time and the next time. As I inculcate this bad pitching habit, I am *becoming* a worse pitcher with each errant throw. Similarly, over time, my actions dictate who I am, because my habits become integral to who I am. And yet, how often do we hear something like: *"Deep down I'm a good guy... despite what I did last weekend"*?

The virtue tradition teaches us the vital truth that we are on a journey of *becoming*. *We are becoming a certain kind of person along the way.* What we're doing each day is developing and fostering who we are, for better or worse. We are moving closer to—or further away from—our *telos*, our ultimate end.

Modernity	*Classical Catholic View*
(separate, disconnected moral dilemmas)	(moral <u>continuity</u> in one's life, through growth in virtue or vice)

o o o o o

HN 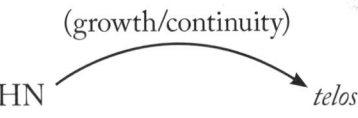 *telos*

(growth/continuity)

Our future self is truly the result of the habits we've built up over time. What we will decide in critical moments is set in motion *now*. So, the moral question before us is not merely *what should I do right now*—but rather, *who do I want to be?*

Imagine if we thought of every decision we made as an answer to that question—*who do I want to be?* We would undoubtedly live with a lot less regret. We might not be perfect, but we'd be far more reflective in terms of where we're going and how we're living—*who* we're becoming.

We do well to imagine ourselves on our deathbed. From that vantage point, what do we think of our lives in the present? What does the hundred-year-old version of myself think of the choices I am making now? These are the questions asked by the person serious about virtue. And these are the questions that make all the difference in where our lives are going.

True freedom is tied up with our growth in virtue—our freedom to love, and ultimately our freedom to be truly happy. This freedom is either growing or regressing by the habits we're forming—it's never stagnant.

So, the question is, *where are we going?*

FIVE
What Are the Virtues?

Virtue enables us to live the fully human life. It's not about suppressing human desire, but rightly ordering desire, rightly ordering our lives, so we hit the ultimate target.

One of my favorite cuisines is Mexican—the spicier, the better! As we all know, the first thing usually brought out at a Mexican restaurant is a basket of chips and salsa. If you're like me, you might find yourself asking for another basket—and then maybe another one after that. Here's the thing—if you keep this up, when the meal comes out, you might find that you are now full.

In a similar way, if we fill up on the "chips and salsa" in life, *we'll miss out on the main course*. So, how do we hit the true target, the *telos*, of a good human life?

Virtue as the Bull's-Eye

As we've mentioned, we are embodied persons. We are a body-soul composite (see *CCC* 362). Mysteriously, the human being is a microcosm of all things, embodying the realms of both matter and spirit. Like animals, we can reproduce. Like angels, we can know and love.

Human virtue is all about training ourselves to seek the good habitually, *especially in and through the body, with human emotions and passions*. Again, it's not about the suppression of desire but its right ordering. Lewis's comments on temperance highlight this: It's "not about abstaining, *but going the right length* and no further."[1]

Virtue is about hitting the bull's-eye, not missing the mark in either direction. For this reason, virtue is the *mean* between two opposing vices. One vice might look like the virtue but is really a counterfeit (called the "counterfeit vice"). At the other extreme is a vice most directly opposed to the particular virtue. As Aristotle puts it, virtue is both a "mean" and an "extreme."[2] As a mean, it lies between two opposing vices, a vice and a counterfeit vice. But as an "extreme," virtue is the *best* and most human—it is the goal or bull's-eye.

Temperance and the Human Person

Temperance is the virtue that moderates our pursuit of bodily pleasure, typically with reference to food, drink, and sex. The vice opposed to temperance is self-indulgence. Another way to miss the mark in temperance is the counterfeit vice of "insensibility."[3] This vice takes the form of an attitude that sees the body and bodily pleasure as inherently evil. This person sees the good life as moving away from the body as much as possible. After all, the body might appear to desire too much food, sex, and so forth. So the easy solution is to wage war against the body—against the flesh—and, consequently, to view the true self as a soul trapped within the body. This, in effect, is to wish one were an angel and mistake what the human being essentially is, viewing the human person as fundamentally a spirit trapped within the body.

This stance is problematic on multiple levels. It tracks with the Gnosticism that beset the Church in the early centuries. Broadly speaking, Gnosticism considers the body and matter as *evil*, and spirit as *good* (the true "self" being the spiritual component trapped within the body). This body-soul dualism led Gnosticism to reject important aspects of the Catholic faith, such as the *Incarnation* (why would God take on human *flesh*?); the *sacraments* (why would God use *matter* to sanctify us?); and the *visible Church* (which is formed through the sacraments, especially the Eucharist). Gnosticism also tended to reject the Old Testament, viewing the "Creator God" as inferior to the true God (after all, why would the real God create the material world and pronounce it "good," as in the opening of Genesis?).

Gnostic sentiments (in their Manichaean variety) led Augustine before his conversion to believe he wasn't even culpable for his sinfulness. At the time, he believed his sin was due to the material part of him and the evil implications of matter—but his "true (spiritual) self" was not at fault.[4]

Historically, this dualistic view of the person tends to move in one of two directions: either toward *hyperasceticism*—a hyper disciplining of the body and shunning of bodily pleasure, i.e., insensibility; or toward *hedonism*—if "I" am fundamentally separate from my body, then it doesn't really matter what I do with my body (as with Augustine above).[5]

This dualism and anti-body sentiment (of insensibility) is also present in strains of traditional puritanism that see sexual pleasure as a necessary evil, something that may be part of the reproductive process but remains nonetheless "dirty" and "unclean."[6] Frankly, a great many Christians today (including many Catholics) have subconsciously assumed this mentality. But this is *not* the virtue of temperance. And it does not stem from a Christian view of the person, as a body-soul unity. The body is good, and our innate natural desires incline us toward *real* human goods,[7] including the pleasure associated with such goods.[8] The trick is to pursue these goods in a *human* way.[9] For example, what is normal and natural for a dog is not so for a human being when it comes to our sexuality.

In the words of Josef Pieper, temperance is "selfless self-preservation."[10] It's the virtue that orders our pursuit of bodily goods so that we can pursue them in a fully human way and not at the expense of higher goods and our ultimate human flourishing. Bodily goods are part of life—even part of a good human life; temperance is the virtue that keeps them from *dominating* our life and preserves our ability to love in the midst of them. Temperance enables us to pursue the rational and human good, even in the midst of bodily pleasures, allowing us to pursue such bodily goods in a thoroughly *human* way, in accordance with our rational and personal nature.[11]

Courage

Like temperance, courage is a virtue lying between two opposing vices. The counterfeit vice is rash boldness. The vice most opposed to courage is cowardice.

Courage is not being without fear; it's choosing not to let our fear control us. There are some things we *should* fear—which it would be irrational not to fear—and true courage is always informed by right reason. Courage is the habit within us that enables us (through practice and habituation) not to cower in the face of difficulty but to stand firm. There are two distinct aspects of courage, manifest in the courage of a *soldier* and the courage of a *martyr*.

Sometimes standing firm means *attacking* and *engaging* evil (like a soldier). Here, confidence and a sense of magnanimity ("greatness of soul") are part of courage, as we believe in our ability to face down difficulties.

At other times, courage calls us to stand firm by *persevering* through an evil that cannot be removed (like a martyr). "Guts" or "grit" captures this aspect of courage.[12] Patience is critical here.[13] Sometimes we can't change a negative situation quickly, and maybe not at all on this side of heaven. Patience (as a part of courage) helps us maintain our peace of mind and composure amid trial, and not lose sight of our ultimate end in eternity.[14]

Courage prevents difficulties or challenges from cutting short our pursuit of the true good. While a healthy fear of certain things should always remain, courage keeps fear from dominating our life and enables us to be relentless in our pursuit of what matters most. For example, especially from the perspective of Christian faith, death is not the greatest evil. Deep in our bones, we know this is true, as we revere and honor those who gave up life itself for something even greater—whether the soldier, the martyr, such as St. Maximilian Kolbe, or the heroic witness of St. Gianna Molla.

Justice

Traditionally, justice is understood as other centered, as giving another what is due him or her, in terms of honor, respect of their person and property, and so on. Thus, justice is inherently *relational*—it's about fulfilling our relationships with others. There are different kinds of justice because we have different types of relationships (e.g., a child and his parents; business transactions; the state and a criminal; a person and his country; a person and God).

In some relationships, we can never repay what we have received, as with our parents. Even if our upbringing was not ideal, we can never repay the gift of life. Here is where filial honor and respect are the best we can do and constitute a matter of justice, a "justice" that recognizes that we can never give back in proportion to what we've received.

In a similar way, patriotism can be seen as an appropriate sentiment, as a matter of justice to one's country. This certainly does not mean that one's country is always right, but it does mean that we have received something from our country that we can never fully repay. For this reason, honoring one's country and its past heroes, and cultivating a sense of gratitude to one's country, are good and fitting as a matter of justice.

Going even further, once we come to see the hand of the Creator, we recognize the force of St. Paul's question: "What have you that you did not receive?" (1 Cor 4:7). For St. Thomas Aquinas, the virtue of "religion" is a subset of the *natural virtue of justice*.[15] From the standpoint of natural reason, once we recognize the Creator, it is "right and just" to offer him thanks and praise, as we say at every Catholic Mass.[16]

Here, we can see religion as a natural good. The human quest for the transcendent God can become muddled and confused with error and human pride; but even confused religion answers to a positive good: we are here at the hand of a transcendent power and ought to acknowledge this in whatever way we can. Accordingly, we should not dichotomize religions as *either* supernaturally true and revealed *or* demonically inspired. Certainly, forces of deception can be at play. But there's also a place for natural religion (or natural expressions of religion) as a positive good, even if imperfect and mixed with error.

Prudence

Prudence has been called the charioteer of the virtues. This virtue straddles both intellect and will. In Aquinas's words, prudence is "right reason applied to *action*."[17]

There are two aspects to prudence—a cognitive/reflective side and an action/execution-oriented side. One can fail in prudence in either direction. If we're carried away by our appetites (and thereby fail to reflect on what we're doing), we become *impulsive*, which is the vice most directly opposed to prudence. But we can also fail in prudence by thinking something to death—sometimes knowing exactly what we should do, but never actually doing it. This is the counterfeit vice of *inconstancy*.

In the impulsive person (overcome by appetite and passion), the failure in prudence is due to a lack of temperance. In the inconstant person (who knows what they should do but fails to do it), the failure in prudence is due to a lack of courage. So, is prudence the first virtue in the order of importance (as the "charioteer"), or not? On the one hand, prudence is needed to identify precisely what the virtuous person should do in a particular situation, and so prudence must lead at the intellectual level (as the charioteer of all the virtues). On the other hand, as we can see here, without the virtues of temperance and courage, we won't be able to execute the dictates of prudence.

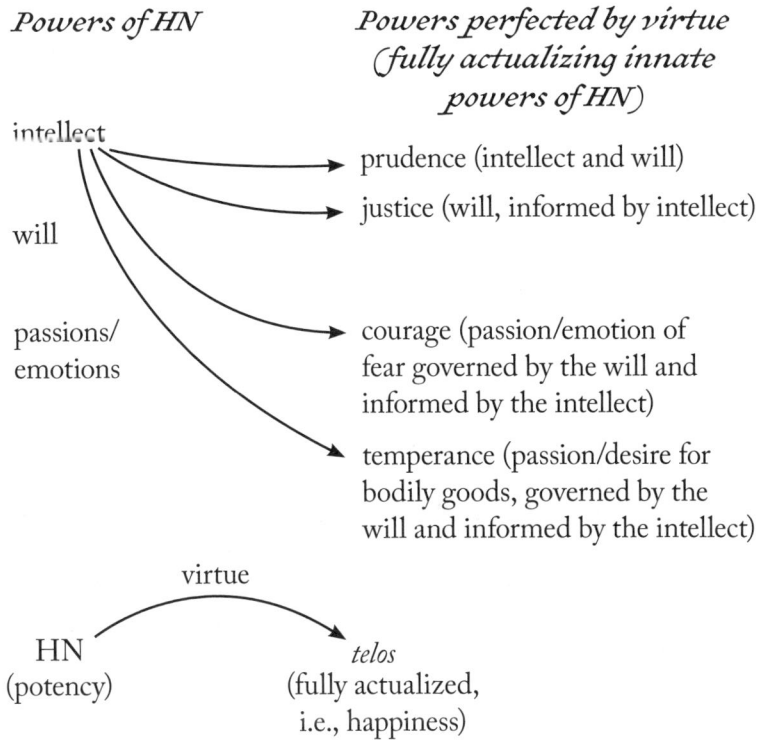

All the virtues tend to stand and fall together. To work on one is to work on them all. But most of us have one or two core vices that beset us more than most. We do well to focus especially on their opposing virtues.

Fear of Suffering

Striving for the virtues of temperance and courage—especially in the beginning—always concerns overcoming some pain. In fact, one can view both virtues in precisely this light, seeing temperance as:
the ability *not to do* what we want to do.
And courage as:
the ability *to do* what we don't want to do.
In this sense, fear of suffering often lies behind many of our moral failures. We're afraid to undergo the pain of refraining from some illicit pleasure. Or we're afraid of the pain of confronting some evil we'd rather ignore. Sin, very often, is a matter of *acquiescence*—we just give up the fight.[18]

But are we ever proud of such moments? The fastest way to bury our self-esteem is to give in to whatever desire comes our way,[19] to consistently take the easy way out. Perhaps for this reason, Lewis sees a special place for courage, as the virtue necessary for all other virtues: "You cannot practice any of the other virtues without bringing this one [courage] into play."[20] Elsewhere, Lewis describes courage as the "form" of every virtue, at its testing point. In his memorable words: "Pilate was merciful, *until it became risky.*"[21]

When virtue is no longer comfortable, popular, or easy, we'll need courage. Without it, our moral efforts soon dry up.

What God Wants

Lewis goes out of his way to show that what God truly wants is the transformation of the human person, the full actualization of our nature by virtue. This is the journey of the human life, of becoming a certain kind of person. He gets at this by distinguishing a virtuous act from the full possession of a virtue, as we discussed earlier. This places the emphasis not just on obedience, but on who we are becoming:

> There is a difference between doing some particular just or temperate action and being a just or temperate man. Someone who is not a good tennis player may now and then make a good shot. What you mean by a good player is a man whose eye and muscles and nerves have been so trained by making innumerable good shots that they can now be relied on. They have a certain tone or quality which is there even when he is not playing, just as a mathematician's mind has a certain habit and outlook which is there even when he is not doing mathematics. In the same way a man who perseveres in doing just actions gets in the end a certain quality of character. Now it is that quality rather than the particular actions which we mean when we talk of a "virtue."[22]

Lewis stresses the importance of this understanding to avoid three significant misconceptions:

First, that it doesn't matter how or why we do the right thing, as if the action itself is all that matters. But the *quality* of one's soul is very much affected by *how* we do something (e.g., whether begrudgingly or with joy) and *why* we do it (e.g., out of vanity or authentic charity).[23]

Second, that all God wants is obedience, "whereas he really wants people of a particular sort."[24]

Third, that virtue is only necessary for this present life. While heaven will be the end of this valley of tears, still, Lewis writes, "there will be every occasion [in heaven] for being the sort of people that we can become only as the result of doing such [virtuous] acts here."[25]

This life is about *becoming* the kind of people who have the capacity for union with God. It's not that God doesn't want us with him otherwise. But there might be something in the very nature of things to consider. If we have not been transformed by virtue, would we even be *able* to commune with God? Would it even be joyous, or might it be *painful*? Is it possible that in the very nature of things, heaven would not be *heaven*, if we haven't become "fit" for such a place? To this question, Lewis writes: "The point is not that God will refuse you admission to his eternal world if you have not got certain qualities of character: the point is that if people have not got at least the beginnings of those qualities inside them, then no possible external conditions could make a 'heaven' for them—that is, could make them happy with the deep, strong, unshakable kind of happiness God intends for us."[26]

Life is a journey toward *authentic happiness, definitive union with God*, and the *fulfillment of our relationships*. It's a journey of becoming—with great continuity in not only this life but also the next.

As an athlete or musician can contemplate their transformation after many long years of practice and take joy in who (and what) they have become, something similar may be true of those who—after having "fought the good fight" (2 Tm 4:7)—will one day wear heaven's crown.

All things worth having come with sacrifice. Why should we expect this crown to be any different?

The first and most necessary steps toward reaching our human end are to grow in the four cardinal virtues (prudence, justice, courage, and temperance), the virtues upon which a good life hinges.[27] This is the beginning and foundation of the story, not the end. The theological virtues (faith, hope, and charity) build upon, perfect, and elevate these cardinal virtues. For example, faith dramatically elevates prudence, enabling us to see the world the way God sees it. Hope powerfully enhances courage, rooting us firmly in the conviction that this life is not the end. And charity elevates justice and temperance, placing all things in the context of love of God and neighbor—empowering us to love God *in* our neighbor and to love our neighbor *for the sake of God*.

In this way, the theological virtues perfect and elevate the cardinal virtues, as grace heals, perfects, and elevates our human nature. The theological virtues uniquely unite us to God supernaturally—either by the light of faith in this life (whereby we see through a glass darkly; see 1 Cor 13:12), perfect union with him in the next life (charity), or the imperfect love and trust that mark the journey of the wayfarer—the one who is on the way but is not yet home (hope).

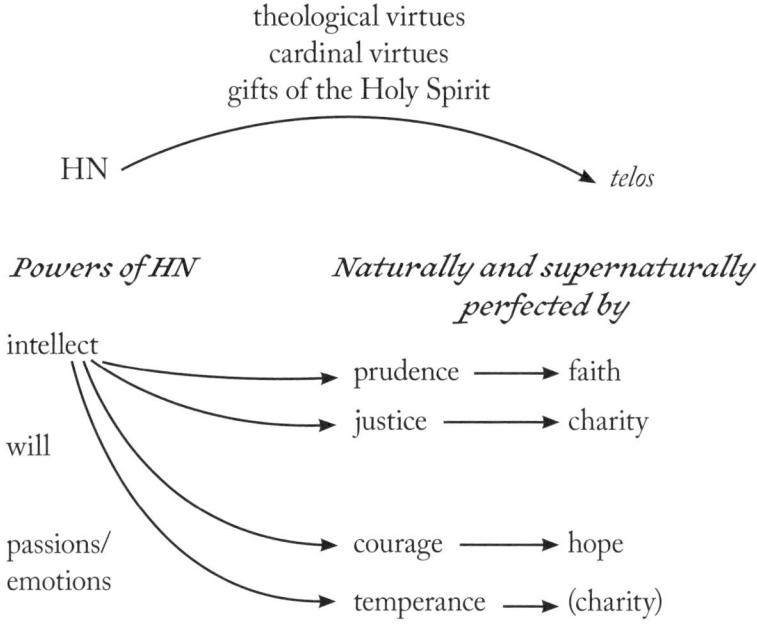

We turn next to Jesus, the one who reveals God to us and reveals most fully what it means to be human. He is the "center of the universe and of history."[28] Nothing could be more vital to our human journey than encountering him, Immanuel—*God with us*.

At this point, we won't be directly dealing with Lewis's thought. Here, we will seek to shore up his work in the face of contemporary objections, particularly those of a historical nature—concerning the trustworthiness of the gospels, Jesus's claim to divinity, and his Resurrection. This will occupy us for the next three chapters.

Part II

ON JESUS AND HIS DIVINITY

SIX

Who Is Jesus, and How Can We Be Sure?

"Who do you say that I am?" (Mt 16:15).

Jesus asks the apostles this question, and it is the same question he poses to every generation. This is the question upon which everything turns. Either the Christian is to be the most pitied of all men, or the Christian has found the pearl of great price—the truth for which our hearts long, a truth that has a *name*—and face—in Jesus Christ.

Preparation for the Gospel

God prepares for the sending of his Son in multiple ways—first, in the Old Testament. Here God's revelation is *gradual*; he doesn't reveal himself all at once. For this reason, as the *Catechism* notes, there are some things in the Old Testament that are "imperfect" and "provisional" (122). There is a typological movement from the Old to the New Testament, a movement from the earthly to the heavenly (see *CCC* 128–129). For example, the exile of the people of the Old Covenant "stands in the *shadow of the Cross*" (*CCC* 710, emphasis added). The Promised Land becomes an image of heaven, our true Promised Land. And the wilderness wandering and the battles fought to attain the Promised Land become an image of our earthly struggle against the world, the flesh, and the Devil (see 1 John 2:15–17).

For the Church Fathers, God also used Greek philosophy (e.g., Plato and Aristotle) to prepare for the Gospel.[1] The same can be said of the "good dreams," that is, the pagan myths, to which Lewis refers: "I mean those queer stories scattered all through the heathen religions about a god who dies and comes to life again and, by his death, has somehow given new life to men."[2] Such mythic stories, for Lewis, point in a shadowy way to their foundational Christian archetype.[3]

If the God of the universe *wanted* to communicate with us, he could do so historically, at a particular time and place, with a people who could receive this communication. This is what Christians believe God has done, most fully by the sending of his Son—by way of long preparation, especially with the people of Israel.

God's revelation engages us as rational agents. He unveils *who* he is (as a Trinitarian communion of persons) and his plans for us in the drama of salvation history (see *CCC* 236).[4] By this unveiling, he gives us the opportunity to recognize, accept, and embrace his revelation—and freely make his plans our own.

Lewis's Famous Trilemma

Lewis is well-known for posing what is often called the "Lord, liar, lunatic" argument. It all stems from the fact that Jesus did and said things that, in a Jewish context, claim divine prerogatives for himself. That is, he claims to be God. For example, when Jesus forgives sins, his Jewish interlocutors clearly take him to be usurping a right that belongs only to God (see Mark 2:1–12). Their response is telling: "It is *blasphemy*! Who can forgive sins but *God alone*?" (Mk 2:7, emphasis added).

The original Greek here literally says, "Who can forgive sins *except the one God [ei me heis ho theos]*?" The Jewish audience is referring back to the Shema, the creedal Hebrew statement found in Deuteronomy 6:4–5 (which was prayed twice a day by ancient Jews), professing their faith in the one God: "Hear, O Israel: The LORD our God is *one [heis]* LORD."[5] In the above passage, Jesus claims to do what only the one God—the God of Israel—can rightly do.

Since Jesus's words and actions constitute a divine claim, Lewis insists there are only three logical possibilities for who Jesus is:

- He is the *Lord* of the universe, as he claims to be.
- He is a *liar*, who deceitfully claims to be God but is not.
- He is a *lunatic*, who claims to be God but is not, unbeknownst to him.[6]

What Lewis refuses to countenance is that Jesus is merely a good man, merely a good human teacher. This view of Jesus has been common at various times and is alive and well today. It attempts to keep Jesus at a respectful distance, acknowledging him as a significant historical figure—but not one who could ever be Lord of one's entire life.

In Lewis's memorable words:

I am trying here to prevent anyone saying the really foolish thing people often say about him: "I'm ready to accept Jesus as a great moral teacher, but I don't accept his claim to be God." That is the one thing we must not say. A man who was merely a man and said the sort of things Jesus said would not be a great moral teacher. He would either be a lunatic—on a level with the man who says he is a poached egg—or else he would be the devil of hell. You must make your choice. Either this was, and is, the Son of God; or else a madman or something worse. You can shut him up for a fool, you can spit at him and kill him as a demon; or you can fall at his feet and call him Lord and God. But let us not come with any patronizing nonsense about his being a great human teacher. He has not left that open to us. He did not intend to.[7]

We must go deeper here because many modern skeptics offer a fourth option: *legend*. In other words, some contend that the historical Jesus didn't even claim to be divine, thereby cutting off Lewis's trilemma from the start. For example, agnostic New Testament scholar Bart Ehrman accepts that Jesus is indeed presented as divine in the Gospel of John, but not in Matthew, Mark, and Luke.[8] By discounting the evidence found in John (which he takes to be unhistorical), Ehrman maintains that the real Jesus didn't actually claim to be divine. Accordingly, it's important that we take up the historical question and that we do so in a full Catholic theological context.

What Are the Gospels, and Why Should We Trust Them?

Recent scholarship has shown that the genre of the gospels is best understood against the backdrop of Greco-Roman biographies.[9] This is important for our appreciation and assessment of the gospels, especially for understanding what was expected from this ancient genre in terms of historical truthfulness. It is worth emphasizing that the gospels are *not* modern biographies. They are ancient biographies—and there's a difference.

Some features of this ancient genre that track with the gospels are:

- Average length between 10,000 and 20,000 words (Matthew: ca. 18,000 words; Mark: ca. 11,000 words; Luke: ca. 19,000 words; and John: ca. 15,000 words)

- Focus on the life and death of a single individual (the gospels focus on the life and death of Jesus)

- Often begin with ancestry (see the genealogies of Matthew and Luke)
- Doesn't have to be in chronological order (that is, they can tell the story of an individual topically to draw out certain themes, as the gospels seem to do on occasion; for example, in Mark, Jesus's cursing of the fig tree [Mk 11:12–14] and the lesson he draws from its withering [Mk 11:20–25] *surround* his actions in the Temple [Mk 11:15–19]; whereas in Matthew, Jesus's cursing of the tree and the lesson drawn from its withering are all together [Mt 21:18–22], coming immediately *after* his actions in the Temple [Mt 21:12–13]. To give another example, much of the material in the Sermon on the Mount in Matthew is spread throughout Luke's gospel, e.g., "Therefore I tell you, do not be anxious about your life, what you shall eat, nor about your body, what you shall put on. For life is more than food, and the body more than clothing" [Lk 12:22–23; compare Luke 12:22–31 and Matthew 6:25–33])
- Doesn't tell you everything about a person (just as the gospels are silent about much of Christ's early life and selective in what they report; see John 21:25)[10]

The expectation of this ancient genre is that the author would tell the substantial truth about the person, but with flexibility in how the story is told. That is, there is an expectation of substantial truthfulness, without the expectation of *exactitude*.[11]

Too often, for us moderns, *when we fail to see exactitude, we think the whole thing is suspect*. But that's not how this ancient genre works—and we should assess the gospels on their own terms, in accordance with this genre and its operating conventions. The implications are enormous. By viewing the gospels as Greco-Roman biographies, we can and should assume that the followers of Jesus are telling us the substantial truth about what their master said and did. But recounting the substantial truth—in this ancient context—does not mean verbatim exactitude.[12]

This comes through in the gospel accounts. Some variant passages are likely due to Jesus having said similar things on multiple occasions, and in slightly different ways (see Luke 6:17–49 and Matthew 5–7). In my own teaching, I've given many lectures to undergraduates on the same topic (or given talks across the country to popular audiences on the same topic)—and no two lectures are *exactly* the same, even when covering the same ground.

But other instances in the gospels can't be explained this way because certain events only happened once. For example, the Father's voice at Jesus's baptism says *substantially* the same thing in Matthew and Luke, but the wording is slightly different:

Matthew 3:17: "*This* is my beloved Son, with whom I am well pleased."

Luke 3:22: "*You* are my beloved Son; with *you* I am well pleased."

Similarly, if we compare the Last Supper accounts, we find that Matthew and Mark are very close but differ in wording from the accounts in Luke and 1 Corinthians 11 (which are very close to each other). Again, *substantially*, all four accounts are the same, but not in terms of exactitude.

This gets to the heart of the matter. The words of institution at the Last Supper were immensely important to the early Church. If the early Church's concern here was about preserving the *substance* of Jesus's words—not exactitude—we should take this as a major cue for the whole of the gospels. The late biblical scholar John P. Meier sums this up well:

> There is real reason to wonder whether the Gospel tradition and the evangelists were all that concerned about the precise wording of what Jesus said. . . . For example, we have four reports of what Jesus said over the bread and wine at the Last Supper . . . and all four versions differ among themselves. . . . Obviously, Jesus was able to say these words only once before his life abruptly ended. . . . We have here a telling datum: the "Eucharistic words" were clearly important to the early Church—witness their four formulations! Yet importance to the early Church guaranteed agreement in *substance, not in exact wording*. If this is true for these vital "words of institution" at the Last Supper, do we have any reason to think that other words of Jesus were preserved with greater zeal for word-for-word accuracy?[13]

Our thirst for exactitude is frankly due to our being children of the Enlightenment. Ironically, as Ehrman points out, this thirst for exactitude is at home both in the Enlightenment and among Protestant Christians of a fundamentalist bent.[14]

As we will see, Catholics have a deeper approach to such historical and biblical questions, because *Sacred Tradition* quite literally carries the text of Scripture to us. The Protestant thirst for exactitude is in part motivated by an attempt to get around (or behind) the tradition, to find the "true" Jesus, unfiltered by tradition. In this respect, the conceptual ethos of the skeptic and the Protestant is often ironically similar. The bottom line is, there is no access to Scripture apart from tradition—there is no access to Jesus except *through the tradition* and the witness of his disciples.

Being a Disciple in the First Century

In an ancient Jewish context, to be a "disciple" (*mathetes*) was literally to be a "student."[15] But this certainly didn't mean going to a classroom a couple of times a week and hoping to pass a final exam. To be a disciple in this ancient setting meant virtually to live with the rabbi. The disciple learned not just the content of the rabbi's teaching, but *his entire way of life*.

I sometimes joke with my students that those who have taken three or four of my classes (over multiple semesters) can often finish my sentences! When I make this comment with such students in the room, they immediately chuckle, because they know it's true. I then ask them to imagine traveling the country for a year (or more) with their favorite professor, watching them give the same intro lecture again and again. When I ask if they think they would remember anything their favorite professor taught, they immediately respond, "Yes, of course we would!"

Suppose this is you traveling with your favorite professor—and now suppose that over the course of this year, your favorite professor frequently sent *you* out to deliver the message yourself. Do you think you would remember the substance of your professor's teaching, as you practiced giving the same message over and over again?

As the saying goes, *if you want to learn something, teach it*. Delivering the message yourself—*with frequent recall*—dramatically crystallizes memory. (I can certainly attest to this as a teacher and speaker; things I have taught and spoken on for years need almost zero prep.) This scenario mimics the apostles' experience with Jesus, as he was clearly an itinerant preacher, repeating many of the same things over and over again—and as with the example above, the apostles are sent out to proclaim the same message themselves (e.g., Luke 10:1–3). All of this makes it more than reasonable that the apostles would collectively retain the substance of what Jesus said and did.[16] After all, how could they not retain the basic gist of their master's teaching after all this?

Memory and Tradition

What the apostles receive from Jesus is far more than just intellectual content. They absorb his entire way of life—what he taught, how he prayed, how he served, and so on—just as we would receive from our favorite professor by traveling the country for a year or more with this person, as implied by our discussion of first-century discipleship. Further, envision your experience with this professor happening in a *group*, with several people traveling the country together with this professor—*having a collective experience.* Thus, the "memory" of Jesus's followers is not a matter of the telephone game. Rather, it is *communal*,[17] shared publicly and celebrated liturgically on a regular basis.

Again, given the scenarios we have laid out, how could the community of his followers *not* retain the general substance of what he said and did? These experiences with Jesus were formative and were rehearsed communally and liturgically. The apostles were constantly founding churches and tending to them, sharing with them the life and teachings of Jesus and training their disciples to do the same. For this reason, we should assume a constant flow of *receiving*, *embracing*, and *passing on* of the apostles' foundational experience with Jesus. This began during Jesus's earthly ministry, and it continued unabated after Pentecost. This communal experience was a constant check on the stability of what was passed on.

What Is Sacred Tradition?

What is the tradition of which Catholics speak? Why is it the case that Sacred Tradition quite literally carries Scripture to us, including the life and teachings of our Lord Jesus Christ? It is important to note that Sacred Tradition does *not* refer to the private teachings that didn't make it into the Bible. Rather, Sacred Tradition refers to the very *life of Christ*—what he taught, how he prayed, how he served—passed on to the apostles and then to their successors, the bishops. It builds upon what we said about discipleship above: The rabbi communicates his entire way of life—his entire being—to his disciples. Sacred Tradition, therefore, is the *life* of Christ passed on in the Church.

It's a mistake, then, to think of Catholic Tradition in an overly cerebral way, as if it merely applied to *teaching*. The *Catechism* stresses that Sacred Tradition is found in the *doctrine*, *life*, and *worship* of the Church:

"This living transmission, *accomplished in the Holy Spirit*, is called Tradition, since it is distinct from Sacred Scripture, though closely connected to it. Through Tradition, 'the Church, in her *doctrine, life,* and *worship,* perpetuates and transmits to every generation *all that she herself is, all that she believes*'" (*CCC* 78, citing *Dei Verbum* 8, emphasis added).

The liturgy of the Church—especially in the celebration of the Holy Eucharist—is the chief custodian of Sacred Tradition.[18] Liturgy is the memory of the Church: *Lex orandi, lex credendi,* the law of prayer, is the law of belief. Though a scandal to non-Catholics, this saying is deeply true: "According to a saying of the Fathers, Sacred Scripture is written *principally in the Church's heart rather than in documents and records,* for the Church carries in her Tradition the living memorial of God's Word" (*CCC* 113, emphasis added).

So, *why* do Catholics believe? Wherein lies our certainty of faith?

Fundamentally, it is faith in the received Tradition, passed on from the apostles and preserved by the Church (see *CCC* 85–86). Here, the Catholic account is both theological and historical. It is rooted very much in the veracity of the ecclesial community that transmits the Sacred Scriptures to us, not simply in the texts themselves as mere historical documents, taken in isolation from the community of faith.

That said, while it is important to have this historical and theological framework in place, we can also make a strong case for the trustworthiness of the gospels as historical documents on their own terms. So, what can we do to bolster our trust in the apostolic witness to Jesus's life and what can we say about the trustworthiness of the gospels, in order to undergird more thoroughly Lewis's trilemma—that Jesus must be Lord, liar, or lunatic?

Who Wrote the Gospels?

Sacred Tradition holds that the four gospels originate with either apostles (as in Matthew and John) or their close associates (Luke is a companion and disciple of Paul, and Mark a disciple of Peter). The earliest witnesses from the Church Fathers repeatedly associate these four authors with their respective gospels, as do the ancient textual manuscripts themselves, going back as far as we can trace them.[19]

For example, St. Irenaeus (writing in AD 180)—who was a disciple of St. Polycarp, who himself was a disciple of St. John the Apostle—writes the following regarding Matthew: "Now Matthew published among the Hebrews a written gospel also in their tongue, while Peter and Paul were preaching in Rome and founding the church."[20] This statement comes from someone who closely knew people who (closely) knew the apostles. Such quotes can be multiplied for each of the four gospels.[21]

Notice that this text by Irenaeus offers support both for Matthew as the author of the first gospel *and* for the date of its composition ("while Peter and Paul were preaching in Rome"). This would place the writing of Matthew in the mid-60s AD, since both Peter and Paul were martyred under Nero in the mid- to late 60s.

What Do We Mean by "Author"?

While Matthew, a tax collector, is the apostle most likely to be literate,[22] we do well to gain clarity on what "author" necessarily means in this ancient context. For example, who wrote the letter to the Romans? You're probably thinking, "*St. Paul, of course!*" But look carefully—he tells us that he used a *scribe* named "Tertius" (see Romans 16:21). Sometimes Paul writes in his own hand (see 1 Corinthians 15:21), and sometimes through a scribe (as here in Romans).

The point is this: What we mean by "author" in this ancient context is the *authority* behind the text. We don't necessarily mean the person who physically penned every stroke. John the Apostle, for instance, could easily have made use of a scribe. In this way, the Tradition of the Church confidently sees the apostles (or their close associates) as the authors of the gospels; that is, they are the authorities behind the text. And this is why we fundamentally trust the gospels, because they originated with Jesus's closest associates, who shared deeply in his life and mission—or were deeply associated with those who did so, as with Mark and Luke.[23]

Besides, *why would anyone make up the authorship of "Mark" or "Luke"?* If it weren't for their respective gospels, they would be relatively obscure figures. They are second-generation Christians—that is, non-eyewitnesses to the life of Christ. For this reason, they are hardly the kind of author one would "make up."[24]

When Were the Gospels Written?

As for dating, even skeptics like Ehrman acknowledge that the canonical gospels are *the only first-century biographies* we have of the life of Jesus.[25] It is widely acknowledged that the so-called Gnostic gospels stem from a later period—and while they tell us much about various strains of Christianity in the late second, third, fourth centuries and beyond, they tell us very little about the historical Jesus. In general, the Gnostic texts show little familiarity with the Jewish world of the first century,[26] are often dependent upon the canonical gospels,[27] and thus show the marks of someone writing far removed (in both space and time) from the first-century Jewish context of Jesus.

In contrast, the New Testament shows intense familiarity with the geographic, political, and religious landscape of the region in the first century, regarding both Roman and Jewish authorities. For example, Caesar Augustus and Tiberius, Pontius Pilate, Herod the Great and Herod Antipas, and the Roman officials that engage with Paul (Gallio, Felix, and Festus) are all real people known from history. The same is true of Caiaphas, the Jewish high priest, as well as Jewish groups such as the Pharisees and Sadducees, all of whom are well-known from ancient history. Thus, the New Testament gives every appearance of coming from people present at the time, giving firsthand accounts of the real-life situation in the first century.[28] Their depiction of Jesus is very much rooted in the Jewish context of the Old Testament and Jewish culture of the time—something decidedly *not* true of the Gnostic "gospels."[29]

Consider the chart on pages 115 to 120 in the back of the book to see how firmly grounded the New Testament is in the historical context of its day. The chart shows numerous figures from the New Testament who have been directly verified historically, either from material evidence archaeologically or from ancient historical sources of the period. Clearly, the New Testament is not "myth," since myth is *atemporal* (that is, not rooted in time and history), as it aims to capture timeless concepts at the heart of a people's identity and convictions. Rather, the New Testament is firmly rooted in the history of its day because it is a historical document, passing on the witness of people directly present at the time.

The standard dating of the gospels (accepted by the likes of skeptics like Ehrman, typically between AD 70 and 90) still places them within the living memory of the apostles and their immediate followers. If the disciples were in their late teens or early twenties when Jesus called them, they would be around seventy years old by AD 80. This would be like a Jewish grandparent around the close of the twentieth century, sharing memories of their time in Auschwitz, a testimony we would revere and embrace as giving us a privileged window into what that horrible experience was really like.

Or perhaps many of us can envision ourselves sharing our experience of 9/11 someday with loved ones a generation from now, say, in the year 2050. Are there any of us above the age of forty who don't remember exactly where we were when we heard the news, with vivid memories of what that day and the days following were like?

Memories in which we are emotionally involved and invested tend to stick, especially when we have continually rehearsed them in our minds and hearts (all the more so when we have rehearsed them publicly and communally in a group on a regular basis).[30] And as the elderly often attest, memory is strongest when it concerns impressionable experiences earlier in life, much more so than remembering what we had for lunch the day before.

Early Dating of the Gospels

There are convincing reasons to place the writing of the gospels even earlier (particularly Matthew, Mark, and Luke)—that is, within thirty years or so of Jesus's death, which would situate the writing of the Gospel within the very first generation of Christians.[31] The first reason is the peculiar ending of the Acts of the Apostles (which is the sequel to Luke's gospel; see Acts 1:1–2 and Luke 1:1–4), with Paul still alive and awaiting his trial in Rome (see Acts 28:14, 30). The end of the book leaves us with Paul serving two years under house arrest, waiting for his trial.

The reader is left wondering: *What happened to Paul? Was he found guilty? Was he acquitted?* It's a strange way to end a dramatic work that directly focuses on Paul's life and ministry from Acts 13 on (with Paul's encounter on the road to Damascus recounted in Acts 9). This odd conclusion is best explained by supposing that *Paul is still alive* at the time of Luke's writing. Since Paul was martyred under Nero in the mid-to-late 60s (Nero committed suicide in AD 68), this would place the writing of Acts in the early to mid-60s—thereby placing Luke (as the first volume) earlier still.[32]

Interestingly, Luke tells us his is not the first gospel written (see Luke 1:1–4); Luke is likely referring to Mark and possibly even Matthew, which would potentially place those gospels even earlier, perhaps in the 50s.[33]

The second reason to date Matthew, Mark, and Luke before AD 70 is that some of the language in the Olivet Discourse (where Jesus prophesies the coming destruction of Jerusalem and the Temple, which was fulfilled in AD 70) reads rather awkwardly, if written *after* the events of AD 70. For example, Jesus says, "Pray that your flight may not be in *winter*" (Mt 24:20). This is odd because the Romans destroyed Jerusalem and its Temple in *late summer*—July/August.[34]

The parallel in Luke would also read awkwardly, as it has Jesus exhorting us not to enter the city when this destruction is taking place: "Let not those who are out in the country enter it" (Lk 21:21). Why include the exhortation not to enter the city, if Jerusalem is already in rubble at the time of Luke's writing?

Both examples would be like someone recounting a prophecy about 9/11 and writing, say, in the year 2020: "When you see the airplanes, *flee the city*—and pray it doesn't happen in the *spring*." It would be very strange to write such a thing after the fact, knowing full well that it happened in September—and certainly odd to offer such an exhortation, knowing it can't do any good, with the event already having taken place. But such a "prophecy" would certainly make sense if it were written *before* 9/11.

Similarly, Jesus's words above read much more naturally on the assumption that the text was composed before the fall of the Temple and destruction of the city in AD 70. Then, the exhortation would make perfect sense, and the comment about winter becomes much more intelligible, since the event wouldn't have happened yet.

Either way—with an earlier dating of the Synoptic Gospels (before AD 70), or with the more conventional dating that places Matthew and Luke in the 80s (with Mark a bit earlier)—it's still the case that one needs at least three to four generations to elapse before one can easily concoct legendary materials, because eyewitnesses (and the living memory of eyewitnesses) need to be long gone.[35] Therefore, the gospels can't be considered "legend" in this sense. That is, in either dating scenario, the gospels are written within the living memory of eyewitnesses.

If someone were to write up something about how Dr. Swafford used to walk on water and perform all kinds of miracles at Benedictine College, there would be plenty of counterwitnesses to set the record straight. Even if someone were to write such a thing forty years from now, there would still be plenty of people within living memory that could (and surely would) falsify such accounts.

That's precisely what we *don't* have when it comes to Jesus. In general, the Jewish response is to see Jesus as a *sorcerer*,[36] that is, one who did supernatural things through the dark arts—much as the Pharisees accuse him of driving out demons by recourse to the prince of demons (see Matthew 12:24). That is, there's no indication from his immediate Jewish contemporaries (or those in living memory) that the gospel accounts are fabricated whole cloth. Since the Jewish leaders desperately wanted to discredit him, this would seem to be very significant.[37]

Considering all these factors, it is eminently reasonable to trust the testimony of Jesus's closest followers and friends—the apostles and their close associates. They give us the substantial truth about what Jesus said and did. We can be confident, therefore, that the gospels put us in touch with the historical Jesus.[38] Our confidence stems (1) from the nature of the ecclesial community that carries the tradition of Jesus to us—publicly and liturgically, as the legacy of the first-century disciples who *lived* with Jesus and absorbed his entire way of life and teaching; and (2) from the fact that the gospels as historical documents come from the apostles (or their close associates) and were written within living memory of the first Christians (and perhaps even during the first generation of Christians, that is, before AD 70).

In the next chapter, we go deeper in terms of historical method and definitively shore up Lewis's trilemma by showing very clearly that Jesus claims to be God in the earliest gospels, namely, Matthew, Mark, and Luke.

SEVEN
The Divinity of Jesus

What Can Apologetics Do?

How should we think of our level of certainty in the context of faith? Can we *prove* the faith? How does a Catholic engage such questions? Apologetics (the defense of the faith) can do two things: It can *remove obstacles*, and it can provide *motives of credibility*, that is, it can give *reasons to believe*.

We must be careful to neither underplay nor overplay the role of apologetics. On the one hand, sometimes people have real questions that pose serious stumbling blocks to their faith. Many people in this situation—including the great St. Augustine—have been immensely helped by serious and cogent responses to their objections; for many, the removal of intellectual obstacles is key to opening the doorways of faith.

On the other hand, many have had the experience of laying out what seem to be terrific arguments, only to find their interlocutor unconvinced (or even uninterested). There may be nothing wrong with the arguments in question, but here is where we must be clear on what apologetics can and can't do. We must recognize that faith is a gift for which we must pray, both for ourselves and others.

St. Augustine's great stumbling block (due to the Manichaean Gnostic influence) was the Old Testament. It was precisely when St. Ambrose taught Augustine to read the Old Testament spiritually that the doors of faith began to open for him.[1] And yet, even though his questions had been answered, Augustine wasn't ready to come all the way home just yet: "I did not think that my own beliefs should be condemned simply because an equally good case could be made out for either side. *For I thought the Catholic side unbeaten but still not victorious.*"[2]

"Unbeaten but not victorious" is precisely where apologetics lives. By answering objections, we can show the faith to be unbeaten. But we cannot force someone's hand. The propositions of faith are not the same as geometrical proofs (such as "vertical angles are equal to one another"). As Lewis says elsewhere, when it comes to faith, God will not use the "irresistible" or the "irrefutable."[3] There's always a way out if we want it badly enough (in a way that isn't true of geometry, for example). The journey of faith always includes an aspect of darkness as well as light, making it a *free* act, which is precisely why it's a virtue! With this posture of humility in mind, we turn to offer historical reasons for our faith. What can reason do to show that the Church's received faith is in fact rooted in history?

Historical Method

So much of the "game" here is disproportionately impacted by the beginning of one's inquiry and how one sets down the rules of research. The field of historical Jesus studies is largely in flux, mostly because of the apparent subjectivity of historical methods that were previously deemed "scientific."[4] Much of nineteenth- and twentieth-century historical Jesus research sought to get behind the tradition of the gospels to the real Jesus—to the bare fact of Jesus, prior to his memory being refracted through the testimony of the early Church. Here, again, is where we see the convergence of the skeptical and Protestant outlooks—namely, that the tradition can't be trusted, and therefore we must peel away the crust of the corrupting influence of the Church to get to the "real" primitive Jesus. But the fact of the matter is that there is no such thing as an "uninterpreted" Jesus. There is no "bare fact" of Jesus that is accessible apart from the witness of his followers, that is, apart from the Church. For the very structuring of memories and experiences of Jesus (from the very beginning) already involves selection and interpretation.[5] As Michael Barber writes:

> It is now recognized that doing history entails wrestling with the social and cognitive factors associated with remembrance. This work has emphasized that the attempt to arrive at an uninterpreted past [which is a shared goal of traditional Protestant and Enlightenment thinking about Jesus] rests on naïve assumptions. Memory does not simply involve retrieving perceptions of the past; it also entails a constructive dimension. . . . *Memory is thus unavoidably interpretive.*[6]

Historical memory is about not just the facts but the *meaning* of those facts. The apostles (and the Church founded upon the apostles) steadfastly preserved the memory of Jesus because of what they believed about him—because of how important he became to them. This is the nature of all history; it tells us about both the past *and* what the present community holds dear. This means, as we have said earlier, that much of our certainty of faith derives from our trust in the veracity of the ecclesial community taking shape in Jesus's lifetime and especially after his death, through the apostles and their successors, who preserved the memory of Jesus publicly and liturgically. There is no access to Jesus apart from this community of faith—apart from the Church. This echoes what we said about the importance of Sacred Tradition in the last chapter and understanding the transmission of the faith through the lens of first-century discipleship in a Jewish context.

Given the importance of this theological framework, we can nonetheless still make a robust case historically for the trustworthiness of the gospels, as we began doing so in the previous chapter with regard to authorship and dating. We can do a lot to show that the Church's witness to Jesus is eminently reasonable and grounded in history. Here, we turn to historical method, for the real Jesus must be the bridge between the Jewish context he came out of and the Christian faith he gave rise to. For this reason, historical accounts of Jesus that can *both* make sense of him in his first-century Jewish context *and* show how his words and deeds became the font of early Christian faith and practice should be privileged over others, owing to their greater explanatory power.[7] We will apply this historical methodology to Jesus's divinity (in this chapter) and his Resurrection (in the next chapter). In sum, the real Jesus must be able to explain how the Christian offshoot emerges from the first-century Jewish tree.

Why Was Jesus Crucified?

It's helpful to begin with this question: *Why was Jesus crucified?*

Here is where the "hippie" Jesus who just taught people to love one another doesn't make any historical sense. Such a Jesus would never have been crucified; after all, the command to "love your neighbor as yourself" is found in the Old Testament (see Leviticus 19:18)—and in context, this command concerns not only one's fellow Israelites, but non-Israelites as well (see Leviticus 19:34). So, what is so *new* about Jesus that the authorities found threatening and even subversive? How did his Jewish followers come to see him as bringing their Jewish faith to fulfillment, and yet in such a manner that led to a whole, distinct Christian offshoot from their Jewish patrimony?

The Charge of Blasphemy

One clue is found in the trial with Caiaphas, the Jewish high priest. It's common to hear that Jesus was put to death for his actions in the Temple, when he overturned the money-changer tables (see Matthew 21:12–13). While this commotion certainly looms large, this is not the charge at the trial. The specific charge leveled against Jesus at the trial is *blasphemy* (Mk 14:64).

To place this charge in historical context, it was not blasphemy to claim to be the Messiah—after all, how else is the Messiah supposed to reveal himself? While from the Christian side of things, we now profess Jesus to be the *divine* Messiah, such was not the general expectation for the Jews beforehand. There were different messianic expectations among Jews in Jesus's day, but they largely swirl around hope for a future royal Davidic Messiah (though some also hoped for a priestly Messiah).[8] That is, this hope is primarily one for a *human* figure, not divine.[9]

Importantly, Jesus has been accused of blasphemy before the trial. We've seen one instance already—when Jesus forgives sins and his interlocutors exclaim: "Why does this man speak like this? It is blasphemy! Who can forgive sins but God alone?" (Mk 2:7). In another place, Jesus states, "I and the Father are one" (Jn 10:30), and the immediate Jewish response is to accuse him of blasphemy: "The Jews took up stones again to stone him . . . [saying] 'We stone you for no good work but for blasphemy; because you, being a man, make yourself God'" (Jn 10:31–33).

The charge of blasphemy indicates that Jesus said and did things that claim divine prerogatives for himself. At his trial, it has to do with his use of Daniel 7:13–14 and Psalm 110:1 to identify himself. Though cryptic, he is subtly claiming to be divine—something Caiaphas and those present at the trial clearly pick up on, leading to the charge of blasphemy.[10]

There are other things Jesus says and does that—against the Jewish backdrop of his day—clearly express his divinity. For example, in addition to forgiving sins, Jesus describes himself as "greater than the temple" (Mt 12:6). In a first-century Jewish context, *nothing could be greater than the Temple other than God himself,* since that's where God dwells (see Matthew 23:21). But that's exactly Jesus's point. He is claiming his own divinity, but in a very *Jewish* way.

The same is true of John 1:14: "And the Word became flesh and dwelt among us." The word for "dwelt" here is *skenoo*, which literally means "to tabernacle." Jesus "tabernacled" among us because he is the new and living Temple (see also John 2:19–21).

Let's turn to a sampling of other New Testament texts beyond the gospels to see how clear belief in Jesus's divinity emerged right away in the early Church. This faith of the early Church (expressed in the New Testament) is the "effect" that the historical Jesus must be able to explain.

Other New Testament Witnesses

In the book of Revelation, Jesus is described as "the first and the last, the beginning and the end" (Rv 22:13). This is important because this is exactly how Isaiah describes YHWH, the God of Israel:

> "I am the LORD, the first, and with the last; I am He" (Is 41:4).

> "I am the first and I am the last; besides me there is no god" (Is 44:6).

> "I am He, I am the first, and I am the last" (Is 48:12).

The book of Revelation makes this connection to Jesus explicit: "I am the Alpha and the Omega, the first and the last, the beginning and the end. . . . I *Jesus* have sent my angel to you with this testimony for the churches" (Rv 22:13, 16).

Something similar is at play in the great Christological passage of St. Paul's letter to the Philippians:

> Though he was in the form of God, [Jesus] did not count equality with God a thing to be grasped, but emptied himself, taking the form of a servant, being born in the likeness of men. And being found in human form he humbled himself and became obedient unto death, even death on a cross. Therefore God has highly exalted him and bestowed on him the name which is above every name, that *at the name of Jesus every knee should bow* [*pan gonu kampsei*], *in heaven and on earth and under the earth, and every tongue confess* [*kai pasa glossa exomologesetai*] *that Jesus Christ is Lord*, to the glory of God the Father. (Phil 2:6–11, emphasis added)

The italicized portion here says of Jesus what Isaiah previously said of YHWH: "To me *every knee shall bow, every tongue shall swear*" (Is 45:23). The Greek Septuagint version of Isaiah matches even more precisely what St. Paul says here about Christ in Philippians: "To me [YHWH] *every knee will bow* [*emoi kampsei pan gonu*]. And *every tongue will confess* [*kai exomologesetai pasa glossa*]" (Is 45:23 LXX). Therefore, St. Paul is saying here of Jesus exactly what was said of YHWH, the God of Israel. This is to make a very exalted claim about *who* Jesus is—it's to identify Jesus with YHWH, the God of Israel.

A final example from St. Paul is found in 1 Corinthians 8, where he refers to the Shema, the creedal statement of ancient Israel, expressing their faith in the one God (which we have seen earlier). Astonishingly, Paul inserts Jesus right in the middle of this reconfigured Shema: "For us there is one God, the Father, from whom are all things and for whom we exist, *and one Lord [kyrios], Jesus Christ, through whom are all things and through whom we exist*" (1 Cor 8:6, emphasis added).

Once again, comparison with the Greek Old Testament (the Septuagint) is instructive. The ancient Shema in Greek employs *kyrios* to translate the divine name (YHWH): "Hear O, Israel, the Lord [*kyrios*] is our God, the Lord [*kyrios*] is one" (Dt 6:4).[11] And yet here in 1 Corinthians 8, in his reference to the Shema, St. Paul uses *kyrios* to refer to Jesus: "For us there is one God, the Father, from whom are all things and for whom we exist, *and one Lord [kyrios], Jesus Christ, through whom are all things and through whom we exist*" (1 Cor 8:6).

These New Testament passages from Revelation, Philippians, and 1 Corinthians (and this is just a sampling) bear witness to the early Church's faith in the divinity of Jesus, at a very early stage. (St. Paul's letters, for example, date largely from the late 40s and 50s.)

This New Testament witness is amplified in the next generation, as for example in St. Ignatius of Antioch, writing in AD 107: "There is one physician both fleshly and spiritual, *born and unborn*, becoming God in the flesh, true life in death, from Mary and from God, at first suffering, then incapable of suffering. This is Jesus Christ our Lord."[12] Thus, the effect to be explained is the clear belief in the divinity of Jesus from a very early period—in fact, as far back as we can trace it.

So, what's the adequate cause that can explain this effect? Is there a way that the historical Jesus—*understood in his Jewish context*—can account for the rise of this faith?

We've already seen this to be the case with a few examples above, but we will continue to add to our analysis below. For if we can explain this effect (the rise of early Christian faith in Jesus's divinity) as having its source in Jesus—in a way that is intelligible in his Jewish context—we will have offered strong reasons for uniting the *Jesus of history* with the *Christ of faith*.

Jesus Walking on Water

Although the historical Jesus certainly didn't walk around shouting, "I am God!" he does slowly unveil his divine identity to the apostles over time—and he does so in a thoroughly Jewish way. Importantly, we should not overlook just how revolutionary this is for the apostles. If Jesus is forced to keep his *messianic* identity quiet because of its potentially politically explosive overtones (see Mark 8:30; Matthew 16:20), how much more is this the case with reference to his *divine* identity.

This is why we shouldn't be surprised to find Jesus revealing himself slowly, even in riddles, as it were, as he tries to get his followers to see more deeply who he truly is.[13] For this reason, to fully appreciate the divine portrayal of Jesus in the gospels, we need to see Jesus's words and actions through Jewish eyes.

We turn now to Mark's account of Jesus walking on the sea, as he recounts Jesus attempting to "pass by" the apostles (Mk 6:48). At first glance, this is a strange comment. After all, where is Jesus going?

Digging a little deeper, we realize that this language of "passing by," in its Jewish context, actually *points to Jesus's divinity*. This language is used to describe Old Testament *theophanies*, moments when the God of Israel made his presence unmistakably manifest. For example, in the Exodus, after the incident with the golden calf, Moses intercedes on behalf of Israel. He asks to see God's glory on Mt. Sinai but is told he cannot—he can only see God's "back" (Ex 33:20–23). In this manifestation of God's glory, God "passes by" Moses:

> Behold, there is a place by me where you shall stand upon the rock; and while my glory *passes by* I will put you in a cleft of the rock, and I will cover you with my hand until I have *passed by.* . . . The LORD *passed before* him, and proclaimed "The LORD [YHWH], the LORD [YHWH], a God merciful and gracious, slow to anger, and abounding in mercy and faithfulness." (Ex 33:21–22, 34:6, emphasis added)

Notice here the combination of "pass by" and the divine name (YHWH)—a combination we also see in Mark regarding Jesus: "He came to them, walking on the sea. He meant to pass by them. . . . But immediately he spoke to them and said, 'Take heart, it is I [*ego eimi*], have no fear'" (Mk 6:48, 50).

Jesus's use of "it is I" is the same expression that shows up in the Greek Septuagint's recounting of the divine name revealed to Moses at the burning bush: "And God said to Moses I AM [*ego eimi*], the He Who Is" (Ex 3:14).[14] In the next verse (in the Greek Septuagint), the divine name (YHWH) is translated as "*kyrios*" (see Exodus 3:15).

It's also the case that Isaiah consistently combines the language of "I am" and "I am he" (alluding to the divine name) with "do not fear"—just as Jesus does here in Mark: "Take heart, it is I [*ego eimi*]; have no fear" (Mk 6:50; see Isaiah 43:1, 10, 25; 44:2).

So, what does Mark want us to see here—with the combination of "pass by" (an echo of the theophany with Moses at Mt. Sinai), an allusion to the divine name (with *ego eimi*), and the use of "do not fear" (a phrase Isaiah frequently combines with the divine name)? That *the God of Israel has returned to his people in and through Jesus Christ*; that Jesus Christ is God in the flesh—he is a "theophany," greater than the theophanies of the Old Testament, when God appeared to Moses or Elijah (the same "pass by" language occurs with Elijah's theophany experience in 1 Kings 19:11). But to see this, we have to see the text through Jewish eyes, to unveil the riddle beneath the surface. Here, we see—in its Jewish context—the historical foundation of early Christian faith in Jesus's divinity.

Jesus claims to be divine not only in John but in the Synoptic Gospels as well, as is clear from these examples:

- Jesus *forgives sins* (Mk 2:5–7).
- Jesus describes himself as *greater than the Temple* (Mt 12:6).
- Jesus identifies himself at the trial in such a way as to elicit the *charge of blasphemy* (Mk 14:61–64).
- Jesus walks on water and "passes by" the apostles (Mk 6:48–50).

This is just a sampling, as many more examples could be given from the Synoptic Gospels.[15] Jesus is thus the true bridge between his first-century Jewish context and the earliest expressions of Christian faith in his divine identity. Jesus did and said things that, in his Jewish context, identified him with YHWH—the God of Israel.

In this way, Lewis's trilemma remains: *Who do you say that I am?*
Lord?
Liar?
Or lunatic?

We turn next to the all-important question of Jesus's Resurrection. This is the ultimate vindication of Jesus's claims about himself and is

God's definitive answer to the human question. The wage of sin is death (Rm 6:23), and Jesus has defeated the "last enemy," death itself (see 1 Corinthians 15:26). If sin scatters, divides, and disintegrates us, Jesus puts us back together from the inside out, body and soul. In his Cross and Resurrection, Jesus's victory is not for his own sake—rather, he goes forth as our head, empowering us (through the Spirit) to do the same.

Jesus took on our humanity to infuse it with his divinity, conquering sin and elevating our humanity to share in his risen life, as the Catechism states here: "The Paschal mystery has two aspects: by his death, Christ liberates us from sin; by his Resurrection, he opens for us the way to a new life" (654). Redemption is, therefore, not complete upon the Cross, for the Resurrection plays a crucial and climactic role in God's victory over sin and death (see Romans 4:25), to which we now turn.

EIGHT
The Resurrection of Jesus

Given the absolute importance of the Resurrection of Jesus, it's not surprising to find it at the center of controversy and contention. For it brings the question of the supernatural directly before our eyes. It forces the question of God upon us, compelling us to give a yes or no to Jesus and his Lordship. No one can honestly remain "neutral" before such a claim.

In fact, the question of Jesus's Resurrection very often turns on the question of God and the supernatural. Some skeptics are quite explicit about this—for them, *the very prospects of resurrection are already out of bounds for historical inquiry.* Consider Bart Ehrman: "It is not appropriate for a historian to presuppose a perspective or worldview *that is not generally held.*"[1] While Ehrman denies that the historian must have "anti-supernaturalist bias,"[2] that's exactly what he's exhibiting here.

Ehrman's skepticism, in fact, begins with doubting that Jesus was ever buried in the first place.[3] For this reason, we turn first to the plausibility of Jesus's burial after having been crucified, in his first-century context, and then to his Resurrection.

Jesus's Burial

What we want to know is whether what we read in the gospels makes sense in its first-century context. Is it *consistent* with our knowledge of the period, in terms of Jewish practice at the time?

Burial was extremely important for the ancient Jews, something witnessed especially in the book of Tobit (see 1:16; 12:12–22). The patriarchs and their families in Genesis also bear this out (see 23:1–19; 25:7–10; 35:28–29; 49:28–33; 50:22–26). In fact, this is why the "dry bones" passage of Ezekiel is so devastating—because the image implies not only death and defeat, but lack of burial (see 37:1–14).

Philo, a first-century Jew from Alexandria, Egypt, offers an imaginative retelling of the Joseph story in Genesis. In Philo's retelling, the great tragedy for Jacob is not the death of his son, but his lack of burial: "Child, it is not your death that grieves me, but the manner of it. If you had been buried in your own land, I should have been comforted and watched and nursed your sick-bed, exchanged the last farewells as you died, closed your eyes, wept over your body as it lay there, given it a costly funeral and left none of the customary rites undone."[4]

In Jesus's day, ancient Jews practiced "second burial," meaning that the body was first buried right after death—and then about a year later, the bones of the deceased were gathered and put into an ossuary (a bone box).[5] In this way, whole families could be buried together (because ossuaries did not take up as much space as a newly deceased corpse). Given this practice, it would have been incumbent upon Jesus's friends and family to know where he was buried, not only to mourn him for seven days (as was custom),[6] but also to secure his "second" burial approximately a year later.[7]

Would the Jewish Authorities Have Allowed for Jesus's Burial?

The question readers may have at this point, however, is this: *What if those who had the power to bury Jesus didn't care to do so—and those who cared had no power to do so?* Importantly, burial for ancient Jews was a point of emphasis not only out of respect for the dead but also to remain in accordance with the law of Deuteronomy. This is extremely significant, as it would have given the Jewish authorities incentive to see to Jesus's burial, regardless of how little they cared for him: "If a man has committed a crime punishable by death and he is put to death, and you hang him on a tree, his body shall not remain all night upon the tree, *but you shall bury him the same day*, for a hanged man is accursed by God; *you shall not defile your land* which the Lord God gives you for an inheritance" (Dt 21:22–23, emphasis added).[8] Here, burial—even for a criminal—was important to the ancient Jews not solely out of respect for the dead, *but so as not to defile the land.* Deuteronomy even commands that the burial happen "the same day" as the execution.

Josephus, a first-century Jewish historian, echoes the importance of this understanding, commenting that even crucified criminals are taken down and buried the same day: "Jews are so careful about funeral rites that *even malefactors who have been sentenced to crucifixion are taken down and buried before sunset.*"[9]

We happen to have the remains of a man named Yehohanan, who was crucified and buried, and whose remains date to the 20s AD—an exact contemporary of Jesus! The reason we know he was crucified is that a 5½-inch Roman nail remains stuck in his heel bone, attached to a piece of wood; the curvature of the nail apparently could not be dislodged from his foot when he was taken down from his cross and buried.[10] Given that the Jewish Sanhedrin initiated Jesus's execution, the onus would have been on them to see to his burial so as not to defile the land (in accordance with Deuteronomy 21:23). If there also happened to be closet disciples on the Sanhedrin (such as Joseph of Arimathea), then their seeing to his burial is all the more expected. Thus, there is nothing implausible about Jesus's burial, as Craig Evans writes:

> Quite apart from any concerns with the deceased men or their families, the major concern would have had to do with the defilement of the land and the holy city. Politically, too, it seems unlikely that on the eve of Passover, a holiday that celebrates Israel's liberation from foreign domination, Pilate would have wanted to provoke the Jewish population and incite Jewish nationalism. Moreover, it is equally improbable that the ruling priests, who had called for Jesus's death, would have wanted to appear completely indifferent to Jewish sensitivities, either with respect to the dead or with respect to corpse impurity and defilement of the land.[11]

If it's reasonable to accept the burial accounts, then what can we say about the Resurrection? What kind of claims can we make in the face of something so sublime and supernatural as the Resurrection of Jesus?

The Resurrection

If Jesus rose from the dead, nothing else could be more important. If he didn't, as St. Paul says, our faith is "in vain" (1 Cor 15:14). As the *Catechism* notes, the Resurrection is both a "historical" and "transcendent" event (see 639–647). It happened *in time*, so it has a historical dimension. But it's an event that transcends time and touches *every* time. For this reason, our goal, as before, is to show the *reasonability* of the Resurrection, knowing that many of our well-meaning interlocutors may find themselves in the position of St. Augustine earlier: The faith may appear unbeaten, but still not victorious in their minds and hearts. This is the nature of apologetics and historical inquiry, especially in the presence of an event as exalted as the Resurrection.

Faith in Jesus's Resurrection (in the first century and today) requires certain background assumptions that allow one to be open to this miraculous encounter with the divine. Otherwise, Christian faith is choked off before it begins. These background assumptions are twofold: an openness to the supernatural, and a familiarity with ancient Jewish eschatological expectation regarding resurrection. The former is necessary for one even to consider the possibility of Jesus's Resurrection; the latter greatly facilitates one's ability to assent to it.

One might think of these background assumptions as like catching a pass in basketball. No matter how good the pass, if we're not looking for it, we're not likely to catch the ball. The above background assumptions make us ready to catch the pass that the Lord throws our way—ready to apprehend and latch onto the truth of Jesus's Resurrection.

The Resurrection in Its Ancient (Jewish) Context

Historically, early Christian faith in Jesus's Resurrection is best seen in connection to prior Jewish beliefs about resurrection, with Christian beliefs about resurrection showing continuity and discontinuity with their Jewish counterparts. This is important. Jesus's *bodily* Resurrection, as it was understood by the first Christians, does *not* track with pagan or Greek thinking about the body and the afterlife. That is, while Christian resurrection faith can be seen as a development and modification of Jewish resurrection beliefs, the same cannot be said with regard to Greek or pagan beliefs.

Consider Plato's *Phaedo*: There is no aspect of Platonic thinking that involves wanting to have one's body back. For Plato, the goal of "philosophy" is to prepare for death, rise above one's senses, and ultimately have the soul leave the body.[12] This is why the proclamation of Jesus's Resurrection (and hope for our own *bodily* resurrection) is such a stumbling block for Greeks in Athens (see Acts 17:32) and in Corinth (see 1 Corinthians 15:12). Consequently, as we will see further below, the distinctive Christian development of Jewish resurrection beliefs—with continuity and discontinuity—becomes a significant *effect* in need of historical explanation. That is, this continuity and discontinuity invites the historical methodology introduced in the last chapter: We must account for how the happenings of Jesus—in his first-century Jewish context—give rise to distinctive Christian faith. In other words, we must account for how Jesus is the bridge from the one to the other—here regarding Jewish resurrection beliefs and their distinctive Christian counterparts.

Christian and Jewish Resurrection Beliefs

First, belief in resurrection was *not* universal among ancient Jews and was therefore not central to Jewish faith. For instance, the Pharisees believed in resurrection, while the Sadducees did not (see Matthew 22:23).[13] In contrast, for Christians, the Resurrection of Jesus becomes absolutely central from the beginning. This is quite remarkable, considering the widespread landscape from which Christians hail by the end of the second century, coming from the likes of Egypt, Jerusalem, Syria, Iraq, Turkey, Greece, Rome, and modern-day France (e.g., St. Irenaeus of Lyon). One might expect this geographic and cultural diversity to influence (and even distort) Christian faith; for this reason, it's all the more remarkable that faith in Jesus's Resurrection becomes so universal, constant, and central to the Christian proclamation all over the Roman Empire (and beyond).

Second, even for those Jews who did believe in resurrection (e.g., the Pharisees), their beliefs are not the same as those of Christians. The Pharisees, for example, believed in a general resurrection of all the just at the end of time, a sentiment expressed by Martha upon Lazarus's death: "I know that he will rise again in the resurrection at the last day" (Jn 11:24). Hence, for ancient Jews, *there is no indication of a risen Messiah in the middle of time*. There is no indication of a two-step process—first with the Messiah, and then everybody else at the end of time (which is exactly what Christians come to believe; see 1 Corinthians 15). This is why Jesus's Resurrection appears so significant to those of a Jewish background: It is an extremely surprising—*though intelligible*—twist upon their fundamental hopes and expectations.

Although we say in the Nicene Creed that Christ was raised "in accordance with the Scriptures" (as stated in 1 Corinthians 15:3), we must take this phrasing somewhat loosely. In hindsight, there is some indication of the Messiah's "death" in the Old Testament—particularly with reference to the "anointed one" being "cut off" (Dn 9:26), but this reference is very obscure. For this reason, scholars of the period almost unanimously assert that there was *zero* expectation of a dying and rising Messiah among Jews of Jesus's day.[14] In the words of N. T. Wright: "At the time, nobody expected that the Messiah would be raised from the dead, *for the simple reason that nobody expected that the Messiah would be killed in the first place*. This was a totally new thing, and it leads us to reflect just a little bit on how impossible it is to account for the early Christian belief in Jesus as Messiah unless something like the resurrection took place."[15]

Historically, we have a handful of other messianic claimants among Jews around the first century, people who claimed to be the Messiah and gathered a following. What we find in every single instance is that *when the leader dies, the movement dies* (or they find a new Messiah).[16] This makes the rise of Christian faith—*after the death of Jesus*—all the more surprising, as an effect that demands an explanation. To turn to Wright once more: "You see, after Jesus of Nazareth had been executed, anybody two days, three days, three weeks, or three years after that would never have said he was the Messiah, unless something extraordinary had happened to convince them that God had vindicated him—something grander than simply going to heaven in some glorious exalted state."[17]

So, the question before us is this: What caused Jesus's Jewish apostles to so radically rethink their messianic categories in the wake of Jesus's death? How did these Jewish followers of Jesus ever come to believe that Jesus—even though dead—was really the Messiah? In other words, how does Jewish resurrection faith get so radically reconfigured around Jesus to give rise to distinctive Christian faith in Jesus's bodily Resurrection from the dead?

The Empty Tomb and Risen Appearances

For Wright, both the empty tomb and the appearances of the risen Jesus are necessary to explain Christian resurrection faith. One without the other, in his view, would not give rise to the gospel stories we now have. Consider solely the appearances of Jesus. Would the mere appearance of the risen Jesus give rise to belief in Jesus's bodily Resurrection—without the empty tomb?

To engage this question, consider the story of Peter in Acts 12, when he is set free from prison and then goes to a house of Christians who are praying for him. He knocks on the door and a servant girl named Rhoda answers; upon seeing Peter, she is overjoyed and runs to tell the others, *leaving him outside*. Their response is telling: "'You are mad.' But she insisted that it was so [that Peter really was outside]. They said, *'It is his angel!'*" (Acts 12:15, emphasis added). Notice here that the mere *sighting* of Peter isn't enough to convince them that he is really there—since they presume him either dead or in prison. They suggest that maybe it's some kind of *apparition* of Peter, but not actually him.

Without the empty tomb—with only the mere sighting of Jesus—the disciples may have had a similar response. They may have thought they were encountering some kind of apparition of Jesus—his "angel," as it were. But based on this experience alone, they would never have come to the conviction that Jesus has been gloriously raised in a new embodied state—nor that, despite appearances, he really is the Messiah. Conversely, the empty tomb by itself would probably lead to the conclusion of grave robbery or desecration, but not faith in Jesus's Resurrection.[18]

Wright contends, then, that the appearances of Jesus *and* the empty tomb are firm historical points; one without the other can't explain the effect—namely, the rise of Christian faith in Jesus's Resurrection.[19] So, what accounts for *both* the empty tomb *and* the appearances of the risen Jesus? What accounts for the radical revision of the apostles' Jewish messianic hope around Jesus? What accounts for the above surprising developments of Jewish resurrection faith among early Christians?

Certainly, the Resurrection of Jesus would do so. It would explain why the apostles so dramatically revised their Jewish messianic categories. It would explain why—even after Jesus's death—Christian faith took off (contrary to other messianic movements of the time). It would also explain why Christian resurrection faith became so universal and central to Christianity, over against its Jewish counterpart.

Here, Jesus's Resurrection is intelligible in its first-century Jewish setting (against the backdrop of Jewish resurrection beliefs), but also becomes the font of origin for distinctive Christian faith. In short, Jesus's Resurrection explains the *discontinuity* between Christian and Jewish resurrection hopes, while still intelligibly fitting within and making sense of those Jewish hopes—to the point that the Jewish followers of Jesus can proclaim that the entire biblical story finds its fulfillment in Jesus and his Resurrection (see Acts 23:6). Jesus, once again, is the true link between the Jewish tree and its Christian offshoot.

With the necessary background assumptions in place (both an openness to the supernatural and a sense for ancient Jewish resurrection hope and expectation), there is nothing unreasonable about Christian faith in Jesus's Resurrection. In fact, it seems to be the *only* explanation that can adequately account for the rise of Christian faith, in a manner that makes sense against its first-century Jewish backdrop.[20]

Jesus's question remains ever before us: "Who do you say that I am?" (Mt 16:15). Given all that we have said, with Lewis, we can say that Jesus must be Lord, liar, or lunatic.

And given that the risen Jesus appeared to "more than five hundred brethren at one time" (1 Cor 15:6)—"most of whom are still alive" (1 Cor 15:6)—it seems quite reasonable that Jesus's claim to be Lord has been vindicated. After all, five hundred people don't have the same hallucination at the exact same time; Paul is clearly making a public claim in the presence of living witnesses—a claim that could easily be falsified, were it not true.

Not everyone will be able to accept the truth of Jesus's Resurrection. Nonetheless, his Resurrection from the dead changes everything. It dramatically announces *who* Jesus is; and it fundamentally alters who we are, especially the nature of our destiny.

We turn next to see the effects of Jesus, starting with the Church. With the same historical methodology utilized here and in the previous chapter, we will explore the founding of the Church and its place in salvation history. Does the historical founding of an institutional Church by Jesus make sense in a first-century Jewish context? Is it possible that Jesus envisioned the Church in any way reminiscent of what we see today? Might there be a genuine link between the historical Jesus and the Catholic Church?

As we have seen, the secular skeptic and the Protestant are generally aligned in assuming that the real Jesus did not envision a visible and sacramental Church.[21] The real Jesus, they often contend, was "spiritual" and "not religious." To this question we now turn.

Part III
THE JESUS EFFECT

NINE
Did Jesus Found a Church?

Spiritual, Not Religious?

Did Jesus envision a Church? Did he envision anything like an "organized religion"? The sentiment of being "spiritual" and "not religious" is alive and well today. Sometimes you see a "Christian" version of this, seeking to embrace Jesus but suspicious that Christian faith could ever entail any kind of ecclesial involvement or regular liturgical practice.[1]

This sentiment does have a positive dimension. A person with such views wants their faith to be *personal* and meaningful; they want a personal encounter with the transcendent. But there is also a negative side, stemming from the danger of wanting to "be our own boss," the danger of self-deception. Sometimes the sentiment of being "spiritual, not religious" results from wanting to preserve our autonomy at all costs while still seeking to retain some of the goods of faith. The danger, then, is that we pursue a faith that merely suits us—one that provides comfort, but never challenges in a way that's unwelcome. This is a recipe not for growth but merely for following one's appetite.

Our question here is this: Is there a way to make sense of the Catholic faith at the historical level, as something Jesus envisioned and established? Is liturgy—especially the Eucharist—foreign to what Jesus gave us, or might it prove absolutely central? As in previous chapters, we want to appreciate Jesus's words and actions in their first-century Jewish context and simultaneously see how his fulfillment of the *Jewish* story becomes the font of Catholic and Christian faith. Again, for the believing Catholic, the Catholic faith is simply the fullness of Christian faith—it's Christianity with nothing left out.

Kingdom Expectation
David

It's hard to ignore the fact that Jesus is constantly talking about the "kingdom of God" (or the "kingdom of heaven"). Let's consider how these words would have sounded to first-century Jewish ears. What hopes would they ignite? Two related aspects of the Old Testament would immediately come to mind for a first-century Jewish audience: the Davidic Kingdom and the hope expressed in the book of Daniel.

God promised David an everlasting dynasty (see 2 Samuel 7:13). The period with David and Solomon marks the high point of the Old Testament narrative. This is called the "United Kingdom" period because all twelve tribes of Israel are united under the Davidic King. The surrounding nations even become part of the kingdom at this point—a universality embodied in Solomon's Temple.

This universality is witnessed in Solomon's dedication of the Temple: He prays that when *non-Israelites* come to the Temple and pray, that the Lord would hear their prayers (1 Kgs 8:41–43). With all twelve tribes united—along with the surrounding nations coming to the Temple to hear the wisdom of God and adore the God of Israel, dwelling in the Temple (see 1 Kings 4:34; 8:10)—this stage provides the earthly blueprint for what Jesus restores and fulfills in the New Covenant.

However, this golden age with David and Solomon is brief, as the Davidic Kingdom divides shortly after Solomon, with separate kingdoms forming in the north and the south. Eventually, the northern kingdom is destroyed by the Assyrians in 722 BC, resulting in the scattering of the northern tribes, who are then intermingled among the nations (see 2 Kings 17). A portion of the Davidic Kingdom continues in the south, until Babylon destroys Jerusalem and takes the people into exile in 586 BC (see 2 Kings 24–25).

We speak of the "Jews" after this exile because they are from the tribe of Judah, the only tribe left at this point. Strictly speaking, "Jews" come from Judah. In other words, all Jews are Israelites, but not all Israelites are Jews.

The great hope of the Old and New Testaments, then, is the restoration of *all Israel, the regathering of all twelve tribes*. This hope for regathering is tied to the restoration of the United Kingdom, the golden age under David and Solomon—with all twelve tribes of Israel united, along with the surrounding nations, worshipping the God of Israel, whose presence dwells in the Temple. This is the earthly template that forms the hope of Israel, which Jesus fulfills in a heavenly key.[2]

Daniel

Daniel was revered among ancient Jews as the one who—in Josephus's words—tells us not only about the Messiah but also *when he would come*.[3] For our purposes, the most important passage in the book of Daniel is the vision in Daniel 7 (which parallels Nebuchadnezzar's dream in Daniel 2). Daniel sees four beasts coming up out of the sea—beasts like a lion, a bear, a leopard, and a terrible fourth beast (see Daniel 7:3–7). These refer to gentile powers who subsequently rule over the Jews. Ancient Jews interpreted these four beasts as referring to Babylon, Medo-Persia, Greece, and finally Rome.[4]

Importantly, according to Daniel, the "kingdom of God" is to be established in the time of the fourth beast (thus, seemingly during the Roman Empire; see Daniel 2:44 and 7:13–14). When Jesus says, "The time [*kairos*] is fulfilled, and the kingdom of God is at hand" (Mk 1:15), his first-century hearers would likely hear echoes of Daniel and the timeline given here.

In the Annunciation in Luke, the Davidic and Danielic hopes are combined, as two ways of saying the same thing: "The Lord God will give to him the throne of his father David, and he will reign over the house of Jacob forever [i.e., the Davidic hope]; and of his kingdom there will be no end [i.e., the Danielic hope]" (Lk 1:32–33).

The Davidic and Danielic passages are set out below, to more easily hear the direct echoes of each in Gabriel's words to Mary:

2 Samuel 7:13–14 (the Davidic promise):

"He shall build a house for my name [i.e., Solomon will build the Temple], and I will establish the throne of his kingdom forever. I will be his father, and he shall be my son."

Daniel 2:44 and 7:14 (the kingdom of God in Daniel):

"And in the days of those kings the God of heaven will set up *a kingdom which shall never be destroyed*" (2:44).

"And to him [the Son of Man] was given dominion and glory and kingdom, that all peoples, nations, and languages should serve him; his dominion is an everlasting dominion, which shall not pass away, *and his kingdom one that shall not be destroyed*" (7:14).

Gabriel's words to the Blessed Mother point to both hopes—the Davidic and the Danielic—as coming to fulfillment in Jesus Christ. This is the backdrop of Jesus's constant teaching about the kingdom of God.[5]

Kingdom and Church: Two Ways of Saying the Same Thing

When Jesus gives Peter the "keys of the kingdom" (Mt 16:19), this is far more than a generic symbol of authority—this is a *Davidic* symbol of authority. When Jesus renames Simon "Peter" and says the famous words, "You are Peter and on this rock I will build my Church . . . I will give you the keys of the kingdom of heaven, and whatever you bind on earth shall be bound in heaven, and whatever you loose on earth shall be loosed in heaven" (Mt 16:18–19), he is referring to a particular office in the Davidic Kingdom, known as the *al bayit* (literally the one who is "over the house"). This person was second in command to the king and had the authority to govern in the king's name while the king was away. In fact, at one point, the king came down with leprosy, and his *al bayit* governed in his stead (see 2 Kings 15:5). This same language is also used to describe Joseph when he is elevated to second in command to Pharaoh in the book of Genesis:

> So Pharaoh said to Joseph, "Since God has shown you all this [the interpretation of Pharaoh's dreams], there is no one so discreet and wise as you are; you shall be *over my house* [*al beyti*, a form of *al bayit*], and all my people shall order themselves as you command; *only as regards the throne will I be greater than you*" (Gn 41:39–41, emphasis added).

The most direct background for Jesus's words to Peter is found in Isaiah 22, where Isaiah speaks of a transition from one *al bayit* to another: "I will thrust you from your *office*, and you will be cast down from your *station*. In that day I will call my servant Eliakim the son of Hilkiah, and I will clothe him with your *robe*, and will bind your *belt* on him, and will commit your *authority* to his hand; and he shall be a *father* to the inhabitants of Jerusalem" (Is 22:19–21). The italicized language here is clearly indicative of an office with authority, even describing this person as a father figure.

Isaiah goes on to describe this office, with words that precisely parallel those of Jesus: "I will place on his shoulder the key of the house of

Did Jesus Found a Church? 73

David; he shall open, and none shall shut; and he shall shut, and none shall open" (22:22).

Here are Jesus's words to Peter, placed side by side with those of Isaiah:

Jesus:	Isaiah:
"I will give you the *keys* of the kingdom of heaven, and whatever you *bind* . . . shall be *bound* . . . and whatever you *loose* . . . shall be *loosed*." (Mt 16:19)	"I will place on his shoulder the *key* of the house of David; he shall *open*, and none shall *shut*; and he shall *shut*, and none shall *open*." (Is 22:22)

Jesus is the Davidic King, and his kingdom is the Davidic Kingdom restored and elevated. Peter here becomes the *al bayit* of the restored Davidic Kingdom, with the authority to govern in the king's name while the king is away.[6]

As soon as this episode with Peter concludes, Jesus begins looking toward his death in Jerusalem: "From that time Jesus began to show his disciples that he must go to Jerusalem and suffer many things from the elders and chief priests and scribes, and be killed, and on the third day be raised" (Mt 16:21). Clearly, Jesus has come to a climactic point in his earthly ministry. With Peter as his *al bayit* in place, he is now ready to die.

Importantly, Jesus's words aren't only for Peter. The *al bayit* is an office, which Jesus restores and elevates. The office lasts as long as the kingdom lasts. That is, *succession is built into the imagery of the keys*. This promise, therefore, is for Peter and all his successors. For Catholics, this is an important foundation for the papacy (formally, the office of the bishop of Rome), who is the successor to both Peter and Paul, both of whom shed their blood in Rome as martyrs.

So, did Jesus found a "Church"? Jesus is restoring and elevating the Davidic Kingdom (and bringing about the fulfillment of Daniel's prophecy). With Jewish eyes, we can see that "Kingdom" and "Church" are ultimately two ways of saying the same thing.

The Messianic Banquet

To get to the very heart of why the Church of Jesus Christ is visible, we must turn to the Eucharist, the Lord's sacramental presence among us. Indeed, in a profound way, "the Eucharist *makes* the Church" (*CCC* 1396, emphasis added). The Church becomes the Body of Christ by her one-flesh union with our Lord in the Holy Eucharist—as *bride*, she becomes the *Body* of Christ.

It's common to hear that the only thing ancient Jews were hoping for was an *earthly* kingdom that would overthrow the political chains of Rome. And this is certainly true of some Jews. Yet there were many other Jews who had a far more eschatological and heavenly hope. We might think of it this way: Virtually all Jews were hoping for a New Exodus, a deliverance even greater than the original salvation God worked in bringing Israel out of Egypt.

If one thinks of the first Exodus as primarily about political liberation, then they're likely to think of the New Exodus as primarily about political liberation. But if one sees something deeper in the original Exodus (as many ancient Jews did)—with the goal of not just political liberation but ultimately worship and liturgical communion with God—then this informs the Jewish hope for a New Exodus, as a yearning for heavenly union with God, far more than mere political liberation.

The Sinai Banquet

The movement from the Passover in Exodus 12, through the Red Sea, and ultimately to the making of the covenant at Mt. Sinai in Exodus 24, is a continuous and unified whole. This is important because the Last Supper tracks with both ends of this Exodus movement. As a Passover meal (see Mark 14:12–25), it connects with the original Passover in Exodus 12—and yet, at the Last Supper, Jesus refers directly to the covenant ceremony at Mt. Sinai when he speaks of the "blood of the covenant" (see Exodus 24:8 and Mark 14:24; Matthew 26:28). Accordingly, the climax of this movement at Mt. Sinai, as the capstone of the Exodus journey, powerfully illumines what Jesus is up to.

At Mt. Sinai, Moses proclaims the word of God to the Israelites (see Exodus 24:3, 7) and then offers sacrifice, saying, "Behold the blood of the covenant which the Lord has made with you in accordance with all these words" (Ex 24:8)—*words that Jesus lifts verbatim at the Last Supper*, as he becomes the sacrifice that seals and ratifies the New Covenant.

But importantly at Mt. Sinai, this movement from the proclamation of the word of God to sacrifice does not end there. It culminates in a *communion banquet meal in the presence of God.* Moses and the elders go up to the top of Mt. Sinai—into God's very presence, symbolic of heaven itself—and have a sacred meal: "They beheld God, and ate and drank" (Ex 24:11). *This banquet meal in the presence of God at the top of Mt. Sinai is the true goal of the Exodus*—which sheds important light on the goal of the New Exodus.

Isaiah and a New Banquet Meal

Isaiah looks back at this original sacred meal in God's presence at Sinai and sees it as the template of what God will do in the fullness of time— pointing to a like but greater banquet meal in the presence of God that will mark the in-breaking of the messianic age:

> On this mountain the LORD of hosts will make *for all peoples* a feast of fat things, a feast of choice *wines.* . . . And he will destroy on this mountain the covering that is cast over all peoples. . . . He will *swallow up death for ever*, and the Lord God will wipe away tears from all faces, and the *reproach of his people he will take away.*" (Is 25:6–8, emphasis added)

Thus, for Isaiah, this future banquet in God's presence is a meal that:

- *Is for all peoples*
- Is marked by *wine*
- *Overcomes death and sin*[7]

Following this trajectory, many ancient Jews hoped for far more than a merely political kingdom; they hoped for a New Exodus that would be inaugurated by a messianic banquet meal in the presence of God— something even greater than the heavenly goal of the first Exodus, even greater than the sacred meal on top of Mt. Sinai in God's very presence that marked the capstone of the Exodus movement.[8]

When the apostles gathered for a Passover meal at the Last Supper and heard Jesus use the words of Moses ("the blood of the covenant"), they may well have thought of the sacred banquet meal prophesied by

Isaiah, as they engaged in this new Passover meal in the presence of the God-Man: a New Exodus, inaugurated by a sacred meal marked by *wine*, which *overcomes sin and death* forever.

St. Ignatius of Antioch (writing in AD 107) describes the Eucharist as the "medicine of immortality, the antidote against death."[9] Here, the Jewish background of this messianic banquet meal (a sacred meal that overcomes death, Isaiah 25:8) informs early Christian faith.[10] It's also reminiscent of Jesus's teaching a year before his death: "He who eats my flesh and drinks my blood has eternal life, and I will raise him up at the last day" (Jn 6:54). Thus, the Holy Eucharist is the messianic food that one may eat and live forever (Jn 6:51, 58; see Genesis 3:22).

The Liturgical Age of the Church

Consider the time span between the original banquet meal on the top of Sinai with Moses and the coming of Jesus—that is, the time gap between the making of the Sinai covenant and its coming to fulfillment at the time of Christ (well over a millennium). In the Old Covenant, this time gap was marked by the ongoing *liturgical commemoration* of the original Sinai banquet meal in the Tabernacle, with the weekly liturgical consumption of the Bread of the Presence, as an ongoing participation in the original Sinai banquet meal (see Exodus 25:23–30 and Leviticus 24:5–9).[11]

Jesus is instituting something similar when he directly lifts Moses's words on Mt. Sinai at the Last Supper. In other words, Jesus here implies a significant *interim* between this moment at the Last Supper (the founding of the New Covenant) and his final coming at the end of all things, when the New Covenant will be consummated in glory.[12] In the New Covenant, this interim is marked by the liturgical age of the Church—through the Eucharist, as an ongoing participation in this inaugural paschal banquet (analogous to the ongoing liturgical commemoration in the Tabernacle of the original Sinai banquet meal).[13]

When Jesus uses Moses's words from Sinai to inaugurate the New Covenant—and then commands the apostles to liturgically commemorate this moment ("Do this in remembrance of me," Lk 22:19)—he signals that there will be a significant amount of time between this moment and the end of all things. Jesus here anticipates the liturgical age of the Church.[14] Thus, Jesus clearly expects his followers to continue after him, forming a community that is built around the liturgical commemoration of this paschal moment.

Not only does this point to Jesus founding the Church—it also points to the importance of liturgy as the heart and soul of this ecclesial community. In the words of the *Catechism* cited earlier, "the Eucharist makes the Church" (1396).

The Eucharistic Kingdom

In Luke's gospel, the themes of *banquet* and *kingdom restoration* come together at the Last Supper: "You are those who have continued with me in my trials; as my Father appointed [*dietheto*] a kingdom for me, so do I appoint [*diatithemai*] for you that you may *eat and drink* at my table in my *kingdom*, and sit on thrones *judging the twelve tribes of Israel*" (Lk 22:28–30). The Greek word for "appoint" is *diatithemi* (both instances above are forms of this verb), which is the verbal form of "covenant" (*diatheke*), a word used by Jesus just eight verses prior (Lk 22:20). Hence one could translate this passage this way: "As my Father has covenanted to me a kingdom, so I covenant [this kingdom] to you."[15]

A couple of important points of background:

1. The only "covenanted" kingdom in Scripture is the Davidic Kingdom (see Psalm 89:3–4).
2. Jesus is the Son of God in two distinct senses. While he is the only-begotten Son, whom we profess in the Creed ("begotten, not made"), he is also "son" of God in the Davidic sense. For each Davidic king became "son" of God (by way of covenantal adoption) on the day he became king (see 2 Samuel 7:14; Psalm 2:7; 89:26).

Jesus's *Davidic* sonship seems to inform the meaning of this passage in Luke. He is, in effect, saying: "As the Davidic son, my Father has covenanted to me a kingdom" (i.e., the Davidic Kingdom). And as the Davidic son and heir of the Davidic Kingdom—here *in the context of the Last Supper*, through the Holy Eucharist—Jesus "covenants" this kingdom to the apostles.[16]

We have here, then, a *Eucharistic kingdom*—a Eucharistic restoration of the Davidic Kingdom. In the words of Brant Pitre, Jesus is bringing about "*the Eucharistic restoration of all Israel*,"[17] referring to the golden age of David and Solomon, with all twelve tribes united, alongside the surrounding nations, worshipping the God of Israel, dwelling in the Temple.

Jesus is the new and living Temple, a reality that continues in his Eucharistic presence among us, as he seeks to draw all nations to himself (see John 12:32). Before the Holy Eucharist (as Jesus earlier said of himself) we can rightly say: *"Something greater than the temple is here"* (Mt 12:6).[18]

When we get to the Acts of the Apostles, as the Gentiles begin to fully enter the Church, the apostolic witness is clear: *The Church is the restoration of the Davidic Kingdom*:

> After they finished speaking, James replied, "Brethren, listen to me. Symeon [Peter] has related how God first visited the Gentiles, to take out of them a people for his name. And with this the words of the prophets agree, as it is written, 'After this I will return and *I will rebuild the dwelling of David which has fallen*; I will rebuild its ruins and I will set it up, that the *rest of men may seek the Lord, and all the Gentiles who are called by my name*.'" (Acts 15:14–17, citing Amos 9:11–12; emphasis added)

Why is the Church visible? Not so much because of institutions and buildings, but because of the *Eucharist*. The Eucharist prolongs the Incarnation among us; that's why the Church is a visible body—because of Christ's ongoing sacramental presence among us. He has not left us orphans: "For where two or three are gathered in my name, there am I in the midst of them" (Mt 18:20). And he is most profoundly present with us in the Blessed Sacrament of the altar.

So, what do we make of the Church—divinely intended institution or human corruption? Against the backdrop of Jewish expectation of the day, Jesus restores the kingdom promised to David and prophesied by Daniel. This Davidic background sheds immense light on Peter's role as the new *al bayit*, showing the Jewish seeds of the papacy. The Jewish hope for a New Exodus is tied to hope for a messianic banquet meal, which finds transcendent fulfillment in the Last Supper and the Holy Eucharist. The Church is the heavenly fulfillment of the Davidic Kingdom: For wherever the king is, there is the kingdom; and *wherever the Eucharist is, there is Christ the King*—a Eucharistic kingdom for those with the eyes of faith to see.[19]

We see here how Jesus's words and actions fit intelligibly against the Jewish backdrop of his day, but in such a way as to give rise to Catholic faith. Jesus taps into the expectations of his day and transcends them, helping us to see how the Catholic offshoot emerges from its Jewish base, as the fulfillment of our Jewish heritage. Appreciating Jesus in his

Jewish context shows him to be the font of the early Church's faith—in his divinity, his Resurrection, and in the divine founding of the Church. Every one of these aspects of early Christian faith represents the surprising—though intelligible—fulfillment of Jewish hopes and expectations. Appreciating Jesus in his Jewish context enables us to see the Catholic Church as the fulfillment of the biblical story, the fullness of what Jesus died to give us.

We turn next to look more deeply at the difference Jesus makes in our lives today. For we don't say Jesus "was," but that he "is"—for we continue to encounter him in the ongoing present, especially in the sacred liturgy of the Church. In the liturgy, time and eternity kiss—*salvation history is made present*. The sacraments, then, become our entrance into this great story. The power of this grace radiates outward into a transformed way of life. As Jesus becomes our anchor and center of gravity, he puts our lives back together, changing not only our interior life but our relationships as well.

The tone of our discussion in what follows will be more reminiscent of the beginning of the book, asking, *what existential difference does Jesus make in our lives today, and how can we more deeply encounter him in the gospels?* As we move into the next chapter, our discussion will draw closely from Lewis and seek to unveil his timeless insights for living the spiritual life today, with confidence, perseverance, and joy.

TEN
The Difference Jesus Makes

Pride: *The* Disease

How do we know if we have a problem—how do we know if we have been infected with the disease of sin, for which Christ Jesus is the only surefire cure?

For starters, how do we handle it when we go unnoticed, overlooked, or slighted in some way? The rub we feel here is the trademark of pride, a deadly and diabolical vice. Pride is not how we feel after we've worked really hard—pride is a radical self-centeredness, a worship of our own egos. We know we have the disease when we lash out to defend our egos at all costs, especially when they are bruised or threatened in some way. As Lewis puts it, "Pride is *essentially* competitive."[1]

Much like a little child, Lewis writes, pride "gets no pleasure out of having something, only out of having *more* of it than the next man."[2] He continues: "We say that people are proud of being rich, or clever, or good-looking, but they are not. They are proud of being richer, or cleverer, or better-looking than others. . . . It is the comparison that makes you proud: the pleasure of being above the rest."[3] This approach to life, as Lewis notes, is essentially competitive. The only way to be up is for others to be down. As such, it is antithetical to love—for love wills the good of the other, such that their good becomes our good. Love *unites* because it overcomes this competition between wills.

Humility, in Lewis's teaching, is the virtue that helps us forget ourselves—helps us no longer vie for our own egos at all costs. Characteristically in Lewis's thought, humility enables us to get outside ourselves and ultimately makes love and friendship possible. He writes:

> Do not imagine that if you meet a really humble man he will be what most people call "humble" nowadays: he will not be a sort of greasy, smarmy person, who is always telling you that, of course, he is nobody. Probably all you will think about him is that he seemed a cheerful, intelligent chap who took a real interest in what *you* said to *him*. If you do dislike him it will be because you feel a little envious of anyone who

seems to enjoy life so easily. He will not be thinking about humility: *he will not be thinking about himself at all.*[4]

In another work, Lewis explains that the goal of humility is to turn our "attention away from self to him [God], and to [our] neighbors."[5] The goal of humility, again, is to take our eyes off ourselves and turn outward in love of God and neighbor. Humility makes us expansive and receptive to the other, enabling us to break out of the black hole of our own egos.

As we can see here, Christian virtue helps us to be better human beings, to become the kind of people who can truly enter the emotional orbit of another and put aside our own concerns and worries, at least temporarily. One of the greatest apologias of the Christian life is the transformation of countless people who have encountered Christ in a living and powerful way and have had their lives changed—people who, after encountering Christ, simply became *better people*. In what follows, we look further at the problem of sin and what it means to encounter the power of Christ's loving gaze and the life to which he calls us.

Threefold Concupiscence and Christian Praxis

What is our problem as humans more precisely? St. John offers an apt summary when he describes a threefold concupiscence, a threefold lust, as it were: the "lust of the flesh," the "lust of the eyes," and the "pride of life" (1 Jn 2:16). In the Bible, lust of the eyes usually refers to greed; we see things and we want them (see Deuteronomy 15:9–11). Here, then, we have three "P's"—three inordinate desires that mark the human condition and lead us into sin: *pleasure, possessions,* and *pride.*[6]

There's an echo of this movement in the garden, when Eve "saw the tree was good *for food* [lust of the flesh], and that it was a *delight to the eyes* [lust of the eyes], and that the tree was to be desired *to make one wise* [wise without God, i.e., pride of life]" (Gn 3:6, emphasis added). Jesus's temptations in the desert engage this same threefold movement: Jesus is tempted to turn stones into bread (lust of the flesh), to receive all the kingdoms of the world (lust of the eyes), and to throw himself down and show off who he really is (pride of life) (see Luke 4:1–13). As the New Adam and New Israel, Jesus here vanquishes the Devil, succeeding where each has previously failed (see *CCC* 538–539).

So, how do we enter into this victory? How do we make it our own? We allow Christ to penetrate us and make us new, something easier said than done! This cruciform way of life takes on a practical hue. Jesus calls us to a life of *fasting*, *almsgiving*, and *prayer* as the antidote to this threefold concupiscence (see Matthew 6:1–18). While Jesus commands us not to do these actions "in order to be seen" (or praised) by others (see Matthew 6:1, 2, 5, 16), he exhorts us to do them nonetheless.

Human condition	Antidote
— Lust of the flesh	— Fasting
— Lust of the eyes	— Almsgiving
— Pride of life	— Prayer[7]

If we are addicted to pleasure, our acts of fasting bring us closer to the Cross. In our almsgiving, we recognize that *gift* is at the heart of everything we are and everything we have. And in prayer, we enter more deeply into the Cross and Resurrection of Jesus, recognizing that Someone is above us.

The best way to overcome a bad habit is more than just *not to do it*—rather, we must replace the bad habit with an opposing good habit. Vices are overcome by their opposing virtues. The same is true when it comes to our threefold concupiscence and our Lord's call to live a life of *fasting*, *almsgiving*, and *prayer*.

Regarding the importance (and difficulty) of almsgiving, Lewis writes:

> I am afraid the only safe rule is to give more than we can spare. In other words, if our expenditure on comforts, luxuries, amusements, etc., is up to the standard common among those with the same income as our own, we are probably giving away too little. If our charities do not all pinch or hamper us, I should say they are too small. There ought to be things we should like to do and cannot do because our charities expenditure excludes them.[8]

When it comes to tithing, for example, it's not so much that God needs our money as that we must learn to detach ourselves from its promises of security. We can even connect fasting with almsgiving; it's fitting for us occasionally to go with less, so that those who go without can have some—or more colloquially, we're called on occasion to *live simply, so others may simply live.*

Why is this so difficult? Are we really that attached to our material comforts, or is it something else? As Lewis observes, it has more to do with where our trust really lies: "For many of us the great obstacle to charity lies not in our luxurious living or desire for more money, but *in our fear*—fear of insecurity. This must often be recognized as a temptation."[9]

Part of the drama and difficulty of the Christian life is that we moderns tend to turn to Christianity *to find support for our own views*, to make us more comfortable where we are—especially when it comes to politics and social life. As many have observed, every group seems to want to claim Jesus for their side.[10] It's tremendously humbling to submit our lives to the scrutiny of what Christian faith teaches and demands. However, to do otherwise is to undercut the power of Christianity at its knees. In Lewis's words:

> Most of us are not really approaching the subject in order to find out what Christianity says: we are approaching it in the hope of finding support from Christianity for the views of our own party. We are looking for an ally, where we are offered either a Master or—a Judge.[11]

Do we honestly *want* to be challenged? In some ways, we are like Bilbo at the opening of Tolkien's *The Hobbit*: A deep part of us yearns for the challenge of adventure, but another part of us would much rather remain where we are—*comfortable*.[12] And yet the adventure—the risk of the journey—is what transforms us. In fact, the journey is precisely how we find the fullness of ourselves. The same is true with the journey of faith: Only when we risk everything do we truly find what we're looking for.

Hope, Mercy, and Despair

The Beatitudes in the Sermon on the Mount consist of a series of "Blessed are . . ." statements. The word for "blessed" here (or "happy" in some translations) is *makarios*. The connotation of this word taps into what we said earlier about happiness; as one scholar proposed, we could translate these passages as, "*Flourishing* are . . ."[13] The Beatitudes give us a portrait of Christ's life and invite us onto the path of true flourishing, by entering into his cruciform gift of love.

The first Beatitude ("blessed are the poor in spirit") points to humility, the foundation of the spiritual life. To allow the grace of Christ to penetrate fully, our hearts must be open; we must reckon with our *need* for grace to allow the Divine Physician to work deeply within us. This is what it means to be poor in spirit—to recognize that our true strength lies not in ourselves, but in God (see 2 Corinthians 12:9–10).

The second Beatitude speaks of mourning. Traditionally, this is interpreted as mourning over our own sin, that is, repentance.[14] Pope Benedict XVI offers a fascinating contrast between the "mourning" of Judas and that of Peter. Both men betrayed Jesus, so the difference does not lie there. Judas's mourning turns to despair, while that of Peter initiates a process of renewal:

> There are two kinds of mourning. The first is the kind that has lost hope, that has become mistrustful of love and of truth, and that therefore eats away and destroys man from within. But there is also the mourning occasioned by the *shattering encounter with truth*, which leads man to undergo conversion and to resist evil. This mourning heals, because it teaches man to hope and to love again. Judas is an example of the first kind of mourning: Struck with horror at his own fall, he no longer dares to hope and hangs himself in despair. Peter is an example of the second kind: *Struck by the Lord's gaze*, he bursts into healing tears that plow up the soil of his soul. He begins anew and is himself renewed.[15]

After Peter's betrayal, Jesus's gaze convicts Peter to the heart: "And the Lord turned and *looked at Peter*. . . . And he went out and wept bitterly" (Lk 22:61–62, emphasis added). We should place ourselves in Peter's shoes, imagining the gaze of Christ turned upon us. This gaze is one of infinite love and demand—of unconditional mercy and a call to greatness.

The Christian life holds two distinct poles together: God is infinitely merciful *and* I am broken. If we focus only on mercy, we end in *presumption*—thinking that we don't really need conversion or change. But if we focus only on our own brokenness, we end in *despair*. Christian hope holds both aspects together, recognizing that we are broken and that God abounds in mercy. Christ's gaze is penetrating and powerful. He sees something in us that we too often fail to see, namely, the greatness of what his grace can accomplish in and through us. In his eyes, we are simultaneously a broken vessel and a masterpiece, even if still in progress.

"Be Perfect..."

By the end of Matthew 5, Christ calls us to "be *perfect*" [*teleios*] as our heavenly Father is perfect (Mt 5:48). This exhortation probably isn't about being sinless; otherwise, it's difficult to square with the Our Father and the petition asking for forgiveness (see Matthew 6:12).[16] Rather, the Greek word for "perfect" (*teleios*), as well as the Hebrew roots behind this word (*shalam* and *tamam*), have the connotation of "wholeness" and "completeness."[17] In context, Jesus calls us to a perfection in love (see Matthew 5:43–48). He calls us to *wholeness* in him. Therefore, we can hear in this passage an exhortation to be *healed* and *made new in him*, so that we can give ourselves away in love.

Our wounds—our unattended shadows—keep us imprisoned within ourselves, hindering our ability to love, resulting in the pride and relentless defense of our egos discussed by Lewis above. For this reason, our own healing in Christ is not selfish but is at the service of our ability to love. To the extent that we fail to enter deeply into Christ's healing gaze, our ability to love and truly enter the world of others is diminished.

The Rich Young Man

This dynamic of conversion shows up later in Matthew with the rich young man, who asks Jesus: "What good deed must I do, to have eternal life?" (19:16). Jesus refers him to the commandments, drawing an essential connection between salvation and the commandments,[18] which the young man acknowledges he has observed from his youth.

In St. John Paul II's reflection, when the young man goes to Jesus, he is in effect asking him, *what's the meaning of life?*[19] Like a lot of us, the young man is basically a good guy. And yet the rich young man knows that he's missing *something*—otherwise, why approach Jesus?

Jesus then says, "If you would be *perfect* [*teleios*], go, sell what you possess and give to the poor, and you will have treasure in heaven; and come, follow me" (Mt 19:21). The young man goes away sad; he's afraid to go "all in" with Jesus—he'd rather just be a "good guy" and keep Jesus at a distance.

There are different kinds of riches and different types of poverty. As we reflect on this passage, we might consider: What am I clinging to in the present that is holding me back from deeper intimacy with Jesus? Maybe it's a relationship, an image we have of ourselves (or one that we desperately try to maintain before others); maybe it's a job promotion we're chasing, or some accolade. We all have different masks and fortresses that we employ to prop ourselves up, to keep others (including God) at a distance.

In other words, we all worship something. Every one of us has an all-consuming concern. The easiest way to see our true priorities—the overarching concern that animates our lives—is to ask ourselves how we spend our *time, money*, and *emotional* and *psychological energy*. This is what we worship; this is what drives our day-to-day if we're truly honest.

As the young man departs, the disciples ask, "Who then can be saved?" (Mt 19:25). Jesus responds, echoing the same dynamic as the Beatitudes above, "With men this is impossible, but with God all things are possible" (Mt 19:26). The heart of the Christian life is a call to perfection in love, one that we cannot attain ourselves. We must become poor in spirit, recognizing our need for God's grace. This humble posture draws down God's grace and beckons him to work powerfully within us, paradoxically enabling us to love in a divine way—to do what we could never do on our own.

The parable of the laborers in the vineyard follows the rich young man in the subsequent chapter of Matthew. This may be a way of suggesting hope for the young man—that he may return by the "eleventh hour" (see Matthew 20:1–16). Such hope remains for all of us. It's never too late, and our conversion is never done. The Lord is continuously turning over new areas deep within our hearts, areas of healing and spiritual growth. Conversion is a lifelong, twofold movement—away from sin (and its vestiges) and toward our Lord.

The Prodigal Son

St. Augustine frames the whole account of his conversion in terms of the prodigal son. As he reflects on his own life, he realizes that going to a faraway land has nothing to do with geography: "No, to be estranged in a spirit of lust and lost in darkness, that is what it means to be far away from your [i.e., God's] face."[20]

One might say that both sons in the parable fail to realize what it means to be a *son*. The younger son is more concerned about receiving his inheritance than having a relationship with his father. Even upon his return, he merely asks to be a hired servant (see Luke 15:17–19). And the older son never refers to his father as *father*. Addressing him, he simply says, "Behold [*idou*], these many years I have served [*douleuo*] you, and I never disobeyed your command" (Lk 15:29). The Greek word *doleuo* literally means "to be a slave." It's as if the older son never truly embraced what it means to be a son, but only slavishly sought to check off his duties. Yet the father addresses them both as "son" (see Luke 15:24, 31).

The heart of the parable is not so much about either son; most of us have likely played the roles of both sons at some point in our lives. Rather, the center of the parable is "the merciful father" (*CCC* 1439). The father sees the younger son far off and "had compassion, and ran and embraced him and kissed him" (Lk 15:20).[21] The father restores the younger son to sonship—symbolized by the robe, ring, and the shoes placed on the younger son's feet: "'For this my son was dead, and is alive again; he was lost, and is found'" (Lk 15:22–24).

This is humanity's story. Closed in on ourselves, we have turned away from God and forfeited our inheritance from the Father. We are enslaved by our own egos—closed off to love and therefore cut off from joy and true communion. Salvation is not merely about avoiding hell, but about the restoration of *divine sonship*, receiving the familial love of the Father and allowing his love to flow through us to others.[22] The culmination of this reconciliation in the parable is a banquet meal, which the Church has long viewed in light of the Holy Eucharist, the most sublime and sacred communion with God—and through Jesus, with the entire Body of Christ.

For St. Augustine, if departing from the father is not a matter of geographical distance, then neither is our return to the Father: "To travel—and more, to reach journey's end—was nothing else but to *want* to go there."[23] The challenge of conversion, as Augustine notes, is to truly *want* it with all one's heart.[24]

As Augustine describes it, his conflicted will resulted in a "fragmenting" of his very self, a lack of integration: "I neither wanted it wholeheartedly nor turned from it wholeheartedly. I was *at odds with myself*, and *fragmenting myself*. This *disintegration* was occurring without my consent."[25] For Augustine, as for the younger son, returning to God means finding not only God *but also his very self*, his true center of gravity. This is the Christian story. While there's a part of us that must die and be purified, what happens on the other side of conversion is that we find our truest and deepest selves. God takes, only to give back so much more.

A critical moment in Augustine's journey comes when he hears the testimonies of people like him, who gave their lives to Christ.[26] As he hears these stories, Augustine experiences something like Peter's mourning above—because these testimonies enable him to come face-to-face with himself. Augustine writes:

> Even while he spoke you were *wrenching me back toward myself* and pulling me round from that standpoint behind my back which I had taken to avoid looking at myself. *You set me down before my face*, forcing me to mark how despicable I was. . . . I saw and shuddered. If I tried to turn my gaze away, he went on relentlessly telling his tale, and *you set me before myself once more* . . . that I might perceive my sin and hate it. I had been aware of it all along, but I had been glossing over it, suppressing it and forgetting.[27]

The heart of the parable of the prodigal son is Jesus's revelation of the radicality of God's love for us, a love that is unafraid of our sin. In my experience, this is the hardest thing about the faith to believe—that the God of the universe cares this much about each of us. But this is the Gospel, revealed to us in Jesus Christ.

It's almost too good to be true—but true it is. Authentic humility recognizes not only our brokenness but also the fact that our sin is not too big for God. While we need to take sin seriously and repent of it, we also—paradoxically—need to be careful not to make *too* big a deal of our own sin (especially after we have repented and received the Sacrament of Reconciliation). If humility, in Lewis's teaching, is about taking our eyes off ourselves and turning outward toward God and neighbor, then obsessing over our failures runs contrary to humility—because it turns our attention back upon ourselves. In *The Screwtape Letters* (which speaks in the voice of a fictional demon about how to ensnare human beings), Lewis writes: "Even of his sins the Enemy [God] does not want him to think too much: once they are repented, the sooner the man turns his attention outward, the better the Enemy [God] is pleased."[28]

We have to be honest about the source of our sadness when we sin. Are we sorrowful over offending the One whom we love? Or is there a part of us that is sad *at witnessing the fracturing of the idealized version we have of ourselves?* That is, is our sadness due to some extent to *pride?* These are deep spiritual waters. The most important thing is to remember that our sin is not more powerful than God—and that in God's providence, even our sins can become the scalpel in the hands of the Divine Physician to work on us and make us new. After all, nothing teaches us our inadequacy and absolute need for God quite like our own failures. Nothing humbles us like our own sin.

St. Augustine once described the dynamic of sin, law, and grace this way: "The law was given that grace might be sought; and grace was given that the law might be fulfilled."[29] The Law of the Old Testament *illumines* sin. The Law exposes how we have fallen short, bringing us face-to-face with ourselves as we come to grips with our shortcomings. But of itself, the Old Covenant Law doesn't give the power to overcome sin. That transforming power only comes with the grace of Christ. Thus, the Law illumines our *need* for grace; and the grace of Christ enables us to do what we could never do on our own—to transform fallen, wretched human beings like ourselves into glorious saints. Sometimes, in God's providence, our own sin brutally reveals our need for grace and opens our hearts to cry out for his grace with greater tenacity than we did when all seemed well in our lives spiritually.

This is the inherent dynamic of the Christian life. If sin brings us to a rock-bottom moment when we truly become poor in spirit, this can become a pivotal step in our spiritual journey—when we finally (maybe for the first time) stop relying solely on ourselves. We become like St. Peter and accept the truth of Christ's gaze—a gaze that exposes our sin and simultaneously beckons us with the most endearing love. The trick is to maintain this humility and deep sense of radical dependence upon God even when things are going well spiritually, not just when sin rears its ugly head.

The Good Samaritan

The Church Fathers often read the parable of the good Samaritan allegorically, offering the following interpretation:

- Jesus is the good Samaritan.
- We are the wounded man, beset by sin.

- The priest and Levite who ignore the wounded man show the inadequacy of the Old Law.
- The inn is the Church.
- The oil and wine refer to the healing power of the sacraments.[30]

For St. John Paul II, the good Samaritan points to the "Gospel of suffering."[31] In addition to its redemptive dimension (see Colossians 1:24), the presence of suffering in others *unleashes a greater love in us* as we seek to ameliorate their pain. The good Samaritan, in his words, doesn't merely stop out of curiosity but makes himself *available*.[32]

In this vein, St. Irenaeus (writing around AD 180) sees us as the *innkeeper*,[33] and the two denarii as a reference to the Holy Spirit, empowering us to live the Christian life: "And the next day he took out two denarii and gave them to the innkeeper saying, '*Take care of him*; and whatever more you spend, *I will repay you when I come back* [*epanerchesthai*]" (Lk 10:35, emphasis added).

Intriguingly, the Greek word *epanerchomai* only occurs in the New Testament here in Luke 10:35 and in Luke 19:15. The latter occurrence is in the parable of the ten pounds, which, like the talents parable in Matthew, is about *what we do with what God has given us*—and *how he will return to judge what we have done*.[34] In Irenaeus's view, Jesus will return to see what we have done with our "two denarii," the gift of the Holy Spirit. In other words, Jesus will return to see how we have cared for our neighbor (i.e., the wounded man).

On the one hand, the Christian life is about grace from beginning to end. On the other hand, as recent research has shown, the language of "gift" and "grace" in its ancient context implies *reciprocity*.[35] The gift of grace—the gift of the Spirit—empowers our reciprocated response, our transformed gift of self in return. This is the "obedience of faith" of which St. Paul speaks (Rm 1:5; 16:26), a life of *faithfulness*—faith perfected in love (see Galatians 5:6).

Therefore, even though the Christian life is about grace from beginning to end, *what we do matters*: "As you did it to one of the least of these my brethren, you did it to me" (Mt 25:40). This is the world-transforming power of the Christian faith, evident in the first centuries of the Christian encounter with the Roman Empire.[36]

Christ reveals to us the radicality of God's love and the transformed way of life to which he calls us. The love of God in Christ Jesus heals and makes us new, so that his love can be poured out through us—enabling us more fully to enter into this cruciform way of life. As we have said, Christ not only reveals God to us—he also reveals us to ourselves. He reveals the truth of the human vocation, to make a gift of ourselves in love—the call to take the transformative and risky adventure of faith, the call to break out of the comfort and safety of our own egos and put ourselves out there before the truth and mercy of Jesus Christ. We can't hide before his gaze; nor, in truth, should we want to. His gaze spares nothing. When we come before him, he brings the whole truth to light—his love and our weakness, enabling us to come face-to-face with where we really are and who we're called to be.

Through the healing grace of Christ, we can enter into the Christocentric meaning of our *telos*. True happiness and flourishing, union with God, and the fulfillment of our relationships come about through *total self-gift*. We are made for communion through total self-giving love, in the image of the Holy Trinity (see *CCC* 221). Thus, the virtue tradition is perfected in self-gift, making possible authentic communion and beatitude. In the words of Karol Wojtyła, the "perfecting of oneself comes through love."[37] Love fully actualizes the person and brings us to our *telos*, especially as we become fully enraptured in divine love. This is the way of Christ, the paradox of the Gospel: "For whoever would save his life will lose it, and whoever loses his life for my sake will find it" (Mt 16:25).

Mysteriously, we truly find ourselves through self-gift. In giving ourselves away in love, we are not diminished but dramatically enhanced—something Tolkien's Bilbo discovers by taking the journey.

In the next chapter, we survey some of Lewis's very practical insights to help us sustain the Christian life, in and through our unique walk with the Lord.

ELEVEN

Growing in the Spiritual Life: Chastity, Forgiveness, and Faith

Knowing Ourselves

Do you ever wonder if we all play with the same deck of cards? Do you ever find that some vices have a stronger pull on you than others, or that your particular cross is not the same as everyone else's? This is no doubt true. Each of us has our own unique walk with the Lord; certain vices (and virtues) will come more easily for us than others. No two people have the exact same journey.

In this context, Lewis discusses the connection between our individual psychological makeup and our moral and spiritual life. He points out that things may look vastly different from God's vantage point than our own. We see only the external; God sees the whole picture. In Catholic theology, this is the distinction between culpability and the objective assessment of a moral act. For example, one can say that a particular act is gravely disordered and even a mortal sin (referring to the objective assessment of the moral act). Culpability, however, refers to one's individual guilt in the eyes of God, which is something only God knows. God alone knows all the circumstances that form the backdrop of a given moment, circumstances that may mitigate our guilt in his eyes (that is, our culpability). Such circumstances don't take away the objective wrongfulness of an action, but they may reduce the degree to which we are individually culpable.

Take, for example, a ten-year-old terrorist. The act of terrorism is objectively heinous and evil, but the brainwashing that must have taken place for a ten-year-old to be engaged in such activity certainly lessens the culpability of the child.

The same is true of those who tragically take their own lives. As the *Catechism* states, "Grave psychological disturbances, anguish, or grave fear of hardship, suffering, or torture *can diminish the responsibility of the one committing suicide*" (2282, emphasis added). One's psychological condition may become so pronounced that the act in question is no longer free or volitional (thus reducing one's culpability). And yet as the *Catechism* also notes, we are "stewards, not owners, of the life God has entrusted to us. It is not ours to dispose of" (2280). While culpability may be drastically mitigated, the action still contravenes the objective moral order established by God.[1]

This is all to say that only God sees and knows the whole story, and we do well to take this into account, both for ourselves and for others. As Lewis writes:

> The bad psychological material is not a sin but a disease. It does not need to be repented of, but to be cured. . . . Human beings judge one another by their external actions. God judges them by their moral choices. When a neurotic who has a pathological horror of cats forces himself to pick up a cat for some good reason, it is quite possible that in God's eyes he has shown more courage than a healthy man may have shown in winning the V.C. [a British medal of honor]. When a man who has been perverted from his youth and taught that cruelty is the right thing, does some tiny little kindness, or refrains from some cruelty he might have committed, he may, in God's eyes, be doing more than you and I would do if we gave life itself for a friend.[2]

This is why Christians are told not to judge: "We see only the results which a man's choices make out of his raw material. But God does not judge him on the raw material at all, *but on what he has done with it.*"[3]

Chastity and the Spiritual Life

One obvious place where many need to hear and apply these truths is with regard to healthy integration in our sexual lives. In truth, self-mastery here is for most people today a work of grace. Sheer willpower tends to have little efficacy. Most who have success in this area have handed their struggle over to the Lord and begged for his help. In fact, this was Lewis's experience. He himself struggled with purity as a young man, but after his conversion found transformation.[4]

In *Mere Christianity*, Lewis offers some very helpful counsel toward this end. First, he insists that we must truly "*want* to be cured."[5] He alludes to St. Augustine, who famously prayed in his youth, "*Grant me chastity and self-control, but please not yet.*"[6] As Augustine pointed out earlier, the hard part of conversion is to really *want* it with our whole heart. So often in this area we want to change, but a part of us is content to remain as we are. We are conflicted and fragmented.

Sometimes we say that we want the *end* of purity and sexual integration. But if we aren't serious about the *means*—the necessary intermediate steps to make it happen—we may be less serious about the end than we claim to be. This battle is won many steps before the fall because eventually all of us reach a point of no return. To genuinely want victory here is to sincerely and wholeheartedly will not only the end but the necessary means as well.

Second, Lewis counsels us to avoid a defeatist mentality before we begin. As he puts it, "Many people are deterred from seriously attempting Christian chastity because they think (before trying) that it is *impossible*."[7] Lewis is right. I've witnessed this on many occasions: People often don't think sexual integration is possible, and for that reason they don't even try. As Lewis says, it's better to have an imperfect answer on a test than no answer at all. Our estimate of what is possible is often skewed: "People quite often do what seemed impossible before they did it. *It is wonderful what you can do when you have to.*"[8]

Third, Lewis insists that we must ask for God's help.[9] We have to depend entirely upon him, and we must be patient—with both ourselves and his timing: "After each failure, ask forgiveness, pick yourself up, and try again. *Very often what God first helps us towards is not the virtue itself but just this power of always trying again.*"[10]

Victory in this battle is a matter of being both tenacious and patient. If this means removing electronics or other sources of temptation, so be it. But victory is not likely to come overnight. And if it did, we might fall into an even worse sin of pride. God is teaching us, even in our brokenness. This process, according to Lewis, "cures our illusions about ourselves and teaches us to depend on God. We learn, on the one hand, that we cannot trust ourselves even in our best moments, and, on the other, that we need not despair even in our worst, for our failures are forgiven."[11]

On the cusp of St. Augustine's conversion, he envisions his old vices speaking to him in a personified way—in a manner that easily echoes our challenges with purity today: "Do you mean to get rid of us? Shall we never be your companions again after that moment . . . never . . . never again? From that time onward so-and-so will be forbidden to you, all your life long?"[12] It's not hard to imagine pornography "speaking" to many today with these very words.

As St. Augustine inches toward his conversion, he begins to learn the lesson emphasized in the last chapter: We can't live the Christian life by our own power. He envisions another personified voice, Lady Continence (who can be understood as Lady Wisdom of the Old Testament, Mother Church, and even the Blessed Mother). After showing Augustine countless examples of others who have trod the same path that he is about to undertake—men and women who were able to leave the debauchery of sin and embrace the purity of the Gospel—Lady Continence offers Augustine both challenge and endearment, much as we have described the gaze of Christ previously: "She was smiling at me, but with a challenging smile, as though to say, Can you not do what these men have done, these women? *Could any of them achieve it by their own strength*, without the Lord their God. . . . Why try to stand by yourself, only to lose your footing? Cast yourself on him and do not be afraid."[13]

To summarize Lewis's counsel regarding chastity and purity (complemented by Augustine here), to succeed in this area we must:

- Really *want* victory
- Believe that victory is *possible*
- *Ask for God's help and learn to depend upon him*

As important as this area is (and sexual sin has destroyed individual lives and whole families), we must see it in light of the whole of the spiritual life. Sexual impurity is not the only, or even the worst, sin. The path to victory here often comes only after encountering the radical love of God—believing, maybe for the first time, that God truly loves us as we are. The life of chastity and sexual integration takes its authentic place within the context of love—God's love for us, and our ability to give ourselves away freely in love.[14]

Forgiveness

When we begin to take the spiritual life seriously, we may be tempted to reduce our progress to a few items on a checklist—a few particular vices (often sexual in nature)—thinking that if these are in line, there's nothing left to accomplish. But over time, in the depths of prayer, other issues begin to emerge, as we get to know the Lord and his plans for us more fully—and as we get to know ourselves more fully, coming to grips with our past and present.

Here is where the healing work of Christ takes on newfound depth. Just as our complexion changes when we sit in the sun, so too the more time we spend in the presence of our Lord, the more we begin to take on his mind and heart, to see ourselves as he sees us (and to see the world as he sees it). In prayer, the Lord reveals to us *the very depths of ourselves*. In prayer, we come face-to-face with ourselves, as Augustine so eloquently noted earlier.

One of our great challenges is inviting Christ into the bitter places of our hearts, places where anger and resentment have long festered. Entering into the healing work of forgiveness may be one of the most difficult—and liberating—aspects of the Christian life. In some cases, forgiveness may not entail reconciliation; it's possible that healthy boundaries may need to remain in place. Forgiveness also does not mean that we *forget* the past, or that we no longer have strong feelings about it. Recognizing this reality helps us to see that forgiveness is always worth it, even if the relationship may never be truly mended.

Forgiveness is fundamentally about *releasing the debt* another owes us on account of having wronged us. In releasing the debt, we free our own hearts from the prison of the past. Ideally, we move to a state where we no longer keep score, no longer stew over the wrongs of the past. This may well be a lifelong journey and will always be imperfect. But it is worth the effort—even more for our own sake than for the one who wronged us.[15] Our healing is at the service of our ability to love, to break free from the prison of our own egos.

In my experience, only in the depths of prayer, slowly over time (and often with the help of counseling and therapy), does one begin to uncover and release these hidden parts of ourselves. Jesus makes all things new, even the most hardened areas within us. This is the journey of the spiritual life, continually going deeper hand-in-hand with the Lord into our own story—because our past lives on in and affects our present. Ultimately, this is a journey of moving from who we are to who we're called to be in Christ Jesus. It's about healing and being made new—it's about cultivating the genuine freedom to love.

The Challenge of the Ordinary

The day-to-day is what our families and loved ones habitually receive from us, making it far more important than we realize. If we don't enter into deep healing with Christ, those closest to us will be the most adversely affected.

The way of the world is to love those who love us. The way of the world is to keep score. But the Christo-form of life calls us to more (see Matthew 5:43–48). We can start by giving others the most charitable read possible. It sounds simple, yet it goes so far. In a pronounced way today, we seem to thrive on hate, as having an "opposition" seems to rally people together *against* someone or something. Do we find our identity more in what we oppose or what we're for? Consider Lewis's trenchant comments:

> The real test is this. Suppose one reads a story of filthy atrocities in the paper. Then suppose that something turns up suggesting that the story might not be quite true, or not quite so bad as it was made out. Is one's first feeling, "Thank God, even they aren't quite so bad as that," *or is it a feeling of disappointment, and even a determination to cling to the first story for the sheer pleasure of thinking your enemies as bad as possible?* If it is the second then it is, I am afraid, the first step in a process which, if followed to the end, will make us into devils.[16]

This can be about news and politics, but it can also play out within marriages and families. If we insist on a negative interpretation of other people's motives and actions, we'll "see" what we're looking for. Conversely, if we actively look for evidence to the contrary—evidence of goodwill—especially among family (or extended family) or coworkers, we'll most likely find positive indications of it eventually. After all, "confirmation bias" is a real thing.

We must be willing to challenge our own story, that is, the emotional interpretation we bring to bear upon the words and actions of others.[17] It's an act of entering into the Cross when we allow our own internal story to be challenged. It's an act of selfless love and can become a fundamental catalyst toward healing relationships at a profound level.

How Do We Sustain the Spiritual Life?

Often, early in our walk with the Lord, we are full of enthusiasm and excitement, which sometimes leads to early (and seemingly easy) conquest over certain vices, as our newfound zeal energizes us. But soon we find that this enthusiasm wanes a bit. We begin to see that the natural rhythm of the Christian life is to oscillate back and forth between spiritual highs and lows. To this point, Lewis offers insightful reflection on the interplay between faith and emotion. He juxtaposes faith and reason on one side, and emotion, imagination, and mood on the other.

We can expect our mood and emotions on occasion to rail against what we know to be true. Lewis uses the example of being sedated for surgery; he knows that "properly trained surgeons do not start operating until I am unconscious."[18] And yet "that does not alter the fact that when they have me down on the table and clap their horrible mask over my face, a mere childish panic begins inside me."[19]

Another example Lewis offers is that of trusting a pretty young woman with your heart (ladies, feel free to flip the analogy!), knowing full well that this young woman has proven herself untrustworthy on many occasions. As Lewis puts it, he is thinking, *Perhaps she'll be different this time.* "His senses and emotions," Lewis writes, "have destroyed his faith in what he really knows to be true."[20]

To give another example, when someone begins a workout routine, they may doubt its effectiveness, wondering if it's worth it. Even if they know intellectually that the routine will likely pay off, there will be days when their mood tells them otherwise. These analogies point to the way in which *faith is a firm and abiding trust in what one knows*, regardless of how one feels moment to moment or day to day. Speaking as a former atheist, Lewis explains:

> Supposing a man's reason once decides the weight of the evidence is for it [Christian faith]. I can tell that man what is going to happen to him in the next few weeks. There will come a moment when there is bad news, or he is in trouble, or living among a lot of other people who do not believe it, and all at once his emotions will rise up and carry out a sort of blitz on his belief. Or else there will come a moment when he wants a woman, or wants to tell a lie, or feels very pleased with himself, or sees a chance of making a little money in some way that is not perfectly fair: some moment, in fact, at which it would be very convenient if Christianity were not true.[21]

Accordingly, Lewis defines this aspect of faith as *"the art of holding on to things your reason has once accepted, in spite of your changing moods."*[22]

In this light, one needs to *train* the "habit of faith."[23] That is, we must *practice our faith*, for what we habitually do affects how we think and believe—how we come to see the world. For this reason, meditation, prayer, and a regular liturgical life are essential to keep the light of faith kindled within us. In Lewis's words, "We have to be continually reminded of what we believe."[24] His point rings true. *We become what we repeatedly think about.* That which we keep private and far from the forefront of our minds and hearts becomes over time less and less real for us.

When it comes to people who walk away from the faith, Lewis aptly notes, "Do not most people simply *drift* away?"[25] If our faith is important to us, "it must be fed."[26] If we don't feed it, we shouldn't be surprised to find it slowly withering and fading over time.

Lots of things are forming our minds and hearts at every turn. For our faith to grow, we must nurture it—by prayer, the sacraments, reading, spiritual conversations, and so on. A powerful way our own faith grows is by sharing it with others. When we do so, we own it, and it becomes more and more real in our minds and hearts.

We're all on a journey, with our own unique struggle and story. God alone knows the whole picture. But sustaining our faith is worth the effort, no matter how imperfect or messy. In so many areas—including and especially this one—the key is to just *keep going*, to just *keep showing up*, even when we don't feel like it.[27] So often, this makes all the difference.

We turn next to the true heart of the Christian story, the true supernatural splendor of what God has done for us. While Christianity dramatically changes how we see the world and how we live, it is more than that. In other words, Christianity is more than just a moral and social program—because Jesus is more than just a good moral teacher who gave us the golden rule. He gave us life in the Spirit, enabling us to share in the divine life of the Blessed Trinity. So, to the supernatural splendor of the Christian story, we now turn.

TWELVE

Mere *Catholicism:* From the Trinity to the Eucharist—and Martyrdom

Today, many think of Christianity as little more than a moral and social program, reduced in effect to being a good neighbor. This reduces Jesus to merely a good moral teacher and makes the Christian life nothing more than a set of behaviors and polite manners. Lewis writes: "For when you get down to it, is not the popular idea of Christianity simply this: that Jesus was a great moral teacher and that if only we took his advice we might be able to establish a better social order and avoid another war?"[1]

This sentiment isn't false; it's just woefully incomplete. It reduces the Christian story to the natural level. As Lewis aptly notes, "If we did all that Plato or Aristotle or Confucius told us, we should get on a great deal better than we do."[2] In high school, I came to a similar conclusion: if Christianity is just about being a nice guy, it wasn't clear what *difference* Jesus really made—after all, Confucius could have taught me that!

What is lost so often in the modern context is the true *supernatural* grandeur of the Christian story, the real difference that Jesus makes—above and beyond the likes of Aristotle, Confucius, or the niceties of polite society.

Life in the Spirit and Divine Sonship

Life in the Spirit, in Christ, is a share in God's Trinitarian life. The great nineteenth-century German theologian Matthias Scheeben once referred to theology as the "study of the communication of the divine nature."[3] He is referring first to the Trinitarian exchange of life *within* God, and then to the outpouring of divine grace outside of God upon creatures like us.

The operations of intellect and will within God are associated with the processions of the Son and the Spirit, the Second and Third Persons of the Blessed Trinity. This is why the Son is referred to as the *Logos*, the Word of the Father (see John 1:1–4, 14; *CCC* 65); and the Holy Spirit is associated with God's love (see Romans 5:5). The Persons of the Trinity differ in their relations to one another; *they differ in the manner in which they possess and receive the divine nature.* The Father begets the Son, giving his entire self to the Son; the Son receives the divine nature from the Father and perfectly images the Father (see Colossians 1:15), giving himself in a bond of love; and the Holy Spirit proceeds from the Father and the Son, as the bond of love between the two. The three Persons are thus truly distinct by virtue of their *relation* to one another. But they are all equally divine, as they each possess and receive the divine nature in a shared communion of life and love (see *CCC* 254–255). In the words of St. John Paul II, "God in his deepest mystery is not a solitude but a family since he has in himself fatherhood, sonship, and the essence of family, which is love."[4]

This is a mystery of faith, revealed to us in Christ and through the outpouring of the Spirit. Indeed, what the Persons do *in* time is reflective of their inner life from all eternity. That is, the sending of the Son (especially in his total self-emptying on the Cross) and the Spirit is reflective of their processions within the Trinity.

This communication of the divine nature *within* God points to the crucial distinction between "*begetting*" (referring to the processions *within God*) and "*making*" (referring to the production of creatures *outside of God*). Lewis writes:

> To beget is to become the father of: to create is to make. And the difference is this. When you beget, you beget something of the same kind as yourself. A man begets human babies, a beaver begets little beavers and a bird begets eggs which turn into little birds. But when you make, you make something of a different kind from yourself. A bird makes a nest, a beaver builds a dam, a man makes a wireless set—or he may make something more like himself than a wireless set: say, a statue.[5]

The Trinitarian processions within God can only be known by faith; they are only known because Christ reveals them to us. Our merely rational approaches to God move from the created order as effect to its unseen cause. But from the effect, we cannot detect the *inner life* of this unseen cause.

Thus, Christ unveils a true secret within God; he shares with us the mystery of God's inner life. But this is not merely a matter of teasing our intellects—for the revelation of the Trinity has a profoundly practical goal. Knowing that God *is* eternally Father of the only-begotten Son illumines how he can really become our Father, too. In the words of Scheeben:

> The doctrine of the generation of the Son of God from the Father provides us with the key to the understanding of our elevation to the status of children of God. Nothing is truer than this; and we need feel no misgiving in maintaining that God has revealed the inner life of the Trinity for the very purpose of enlightening us concerning our supernatural relationship to Him. He makes Himself known to us not only as God but as Father, that we may realize how and why He can be and wills to be our Father also.[6]

As mentioned, the Persons within God who *proceed* are also *sent* into time—these are the *missions* of the Son (in the Incarnation) and the Spirit (at Pentecost). In this way, the life of the Trinity goes outside of itself, sharing this divine life with creatures, ultimately making us true sons and daughters of the Father—enabling us to share in the life of the only-begotten Son. That is, what the Son has eternally by nature we come to share in by grace—*such that God loves us as he loves his only-begotten Son*. This claim is so astounding that it should make us shudder. But it is the truth of the Gospel, so long as we always remember that the glory of divine grace is one of *participation*—a sharing in by grace of what the Son has by nature.

The Holy Spirit, as the culmination of the processions within the Trinity, is poured into our hearts (see Romans 5:5). Thus, astonishingly, what begins as a procession of divine life *within* God is communicated to us: "By virtue of our Baptism, the first sacrament of the faith, the Holy Spirit in the Church communicates to us, *intimately* and *personally*, *the life that originates in the Father and is offered to us in the Son*" (*CCC* 683, emphasis added). For this reason, Christianity cannot be simply about being "a nice guy"—*it's about sharing in divine life*, the very life shared between the Father, Son, and Holy Spirit from all eternity.

The Glory of the Incarnation and Divine Grace

Jesus is the marriage of humanity and divinity; and the Incarnation establishes a connection between the Eternal Son and all humanity.[7] Yet we must appropriate this glorious marriage for ourselves by our yes. We have to accept this gracious offer of salvation—not only of forgiveness, *but of the divinization of our humanity*, so that we can truly become sons and daughters in the Son.

The *Catechism* gets at this when it offers four reasons for why God became man. The first three are to reconcile us to God and atone for sin; to show us the radicality of God's love; and to be our model of holiness (*CCC* 457–459). The fourth reason for the Incarnation is that we may share in divine life. It is worth quoting in full, as the *Catechism* quotes successively from Sts. Irenaeus, Athanasius, and Thomas Aquinas (after citing 2 Peter 1:4). This teaching will appear shocking, but it is the authentic patrimony of Christian faith:

> The Word became flesh to make us "partakers of the divine nature" [2 Pt 1:4]. "For this is why the Word became man, and the Son of God became the Son of man: so that man, by entering into communion with the Word and thus receiving divine sonship, might become a son of God" [Irenaeus]. "For the Son of God became man so that we might become God" [Athanasius]. "The only-begotten Son of God, wanting to make us sharers in his divinity, assumed our nature, so that he, made man, might make men gods" [Thomas Aquinas]. (*CCC* 460)

To capture this divinizing effect of grace, Lewis draws on a distinction between two Greek words, *bios* and *zoe*. The latter is the word used, for example, in John's gospel to describe eternal life (see John 3:16). Both words mean "life" but at two distinct levels—the former refers to *natural* life, and the latter to *supernatural* life in the Spirit:

> Bios has, to be sure, a certain shadowy or symbolic resemblance to Zoe: but only the sort of resemblance there is between a photo and a place, or a statue and a man. A man who changed from having Bios to having Zoe would have gone through as big a change as a statue which changed from being a carved stone to being a real man. *And that is precisely what Christianity is about.*[8]

The following scenario may help us grasp the significance of this divine sonship. Imagine that your car mechanic completely rips you off, and then months later apologizes to you. Forgiving him would be one thing. But then, imagine if you were to not only forgive him but also go on to invite him over for dinner; and suppose you didn't stop there—*you invited him into your family and formally adopted him as your son*, writing his name into your will, enabling him to inherit alongside your other children.

This would be crazy, right?

But this is exactly what God has done for us. Even more than merely forgiving us, he makes us his sons and daughters in and through the Eternal Son: "See what love the Father has given us, that we should be called children of God; and so we are" (1 Jn 3:1; see also Romans 8:14–16).[9]

As we stated above, *what Jesus has eternally by nature, we share in by grace*. This is the Gospel—which is far more than a mere moral code, and far more even than the forgiveness of our sins or a divine acquittal. By nature, we are creatures and servants of the Creator.[10] It is only by grace—in Christ—that we truly become sons and daughters in the Son. The Christian life, from beginning to end, is a supernatural participation in the life of the Son, through the Spirit. Astoundingly, as we are incorporated into the life of the only-begotten Son, the Father looks upon us and loves us *as he loves his only-begotten Son*.

I know my students are getting this when they realize that *moral perfection in the natural order can't earn one bit of this divine life*. The highest of the angels can't earn one ounce of this glorious grace. This is precisely why we cannot reduce Christianity to merely a moral system. Christianity is about *supernaturally* sharing in Trinitarian life, in a way that absolutely transcends the capacities of our nature. This means that our question should never be, "What's the least I have to do to avoid hell?" but "How much of the divine life do I want?"

The Eucharist and the Incarnation

In Lewis's words, the Church exists *for the sake of this divine sonship*—to enable us to become "little Christs." "The Church exists for nothing else but to draw men into Christ, to make them little Christs. If they are not doing that, all the cathedrals, clergy, missions, sermons, even the Bible itself, are simply a waste of time. God became Man for no other purpose. It is even doubtful, you know, whether the whole universe was created for any other purpose."[11]

God became man to do more than just teach us; he took on our humanity to enable us to share in his divinity. But he doesn't do this in a merely disembodied way—in a merely spiritual way. Rather, he became man in the Incarnation, uniting himself to us *physically*, in a manner befitting our corporeal nature.

Here is where the Eucharist extends this movement of God going out from himself and becoming incarnate—for *the Eucharist prolongs the*

Incarnation. Accordingly, the Eucharist brings us into the inner heart of the Trinity, as God goes out of himself and draws us back to him. In the words of Scheeben:

> The Eucharistic presence of Christ is in itself a *reflection and extension of His incarnation*. . . . The mystery of grace . . . is but an imitation and continuation of the mystery of the Trinity [i.e., a share in the Son's "begetting" over and above the mere "making" of creatures], with which it is connected by the Incarnation. Hence the Eucharist, as the extension of the Incarnation, must also bring us into close relationship with the Trinity.[12]

Through the Eucharist, our divine sonship reaches new, sublime heights, *as we share in Christ's filial relation to the Father*:

> As a result of the Incarnation we are no longer merely adopted children of God. Through the sacred humanity [of Christ] we are received into the natural, only-begotten Son of God as His members, *and as His members share in His personal relationship to the Father*. . . . And so in virtue of the Eucharist we do not merely receive our life from God . . . *we live in God*; we have our life from His substance and in His substance.[13]

Recapitulation in Christ—Sharing in His Total Self-Gift

The Eucharist brings us most fully into the life of the Son and associates us with his paschal sacrifice, the Son's unique offering of himself to the Father, made present in every Mass.[14] For this reason, the Eucharist becomes the offering not just of Christ the Head but of the entire Body of Christ (see *CCC* 1368). We should embrace this truth at every level. When the gifts are brought forth, we should envision our entire lives being placed on the altar—our sufferings, trials, joys, hopes, dreams, fears, and so on. We are being offered up *in, with, and through* Christ to the Father.

This brings us to the very essence of Christianity: *for the Holy Spirit to reproduce the life, death, and Resurrection of Jesus Christ in and through each one of us*. This begins in our Baptism, as we are baptized into his death and Resurrection (see Romans 6:3–4); it continues through the Spirit's ongoing transformation of our lives, and it culminates in the Holy Eucharist. And it finds its definitive completion in our *martyrdom*.

For some, like St. Ignatius of Antioch, this is a "red" (blood) martyrdom—which, in his words, makes him a *complete* disciple.[15] For many others, it's a "white" martyrdom, the daily death to self, as we grow in our ability to enter Christ's self-offering by making a gift of our lives in love—that "he may increase and we may decrease" (Jn 3:30).

The Christian story is about love, about entering into Christ's self-offering, the Christo-form of life. This movement is prefigured in the Old Testament and finds fulfillment in Christ. And as we enter into the Paschal Mystery of the Cross and Resurrection, it is being reproduced in us.

Liturgy, Martyrdom, and Sacrifice

The sacrifices of ancient Israel are *ritualized self-offerings*.[16] In fact, *martyrdom*—the quintessential gift of self—is later described *as a liturgical sacrifice*, as is witnessed here in the prayer of Azariah in the book of Daniel, as he faces the prospect of death in a fiery furnace:

> At this time there is no prince, or prophet, or leader, no burnt offering, or sacrifice, or oblation, or incense [because the Temple had been destroyed], no place to make an offering before you or to find mercy. Yet with a contrite heart and a humble spirit *may we be accepted, as though it were with burnt offerings of rams and bulls . . . such may our sacrifice be in your sight this day.* (Dn 3:15–16, italicized found only in the Septuagint)[17]

A similar understanding is found in the book of Wisdom:

> The souls of the righteous are in the hand of God . . . their hope is full of immortality. Having been disciplined a little, they will receive great good, because God tested them and found them worthy of himself; like gold in the furnace he tried them, and *like a sacrificial burnt offering he accepted them*. (Ws 3:1, 4–6, emphasis added)

This theme is also present in the deaths of the Maccabean brothers in 2 Maccabees 7, especially in the words of the youngest brother, who describes their martyrdom as having an *atoning* quality: "I, like my brothers, give up body and life for the laws of our fathers, appealing to God to show mercy soon to our nation . . . *and through me and my brothers to bring to an end the wrath of the Almighty which has justly fallen on our whole nation*" (2 Mc 7:37–38, emphasis added).

All of this is a precursor to Christ's definitive self-offering, as well as the mysterious passage in Colossians where St. Paul speaks of our redemptive participation in Christ's sufferings: "Now I rejoice in my sufferings for your sake, *and in my flesh I complete what is lacking in Christ's afflictions* for the sake of his body, that is, the Church" (Col 1:24, emphasis added). Nothing is lacking in Christ's afflictions on the Cross. *What is left is for the entire Paschal Mystery to be reproduced in and through each and every one of us*, in and through the entire Body of Christ, the Church.

The Christian story is about love—a love rooted within the very heart of the Trinity, which has been "poured into our hearts through the Holy Spirit" (Rom 5:5). God is a communion of Persons, whose eternal love and communication of the divine nature does not hurt. But when the Son continues to love in this divine way—in finite flesh and in a fallen world—*it takes the shape of the Cross* (see John 15:13). Our participation in this path will be no different.

Thus, there is a symmetry between Christ's self-emptying on the Cross and the total exchange of life and love within the Trinity—a symmetry that exemplifies the Christian vocation: "God himself is an eternal exchange of love, Father, Son, and Holy Spirit, *and he has destined us to share in that exchange*" (*CCC* 221, emphasis added).

In this way, we see that the moral aspect of the Christian story has far deeper roots than modern man could ever imagine. Through Christ, the wellsprings of divine life surge within us, recapitulating Christ's total self-gift in and through us, as St. Paul so eloquently states: "I have been crucified with Christ; it is no longer I who live, but Christ who lives in me" (Gal 2:20).

If we let Christianity be itself, it can't help but speak the language of love. But this love always passes by way of the Cross. And this love finds its source in the Blessed Trinity, coming to us through Christ in the Incarnation and especially in the Holy Eucharist. From the Eucharist, it leads to our total gift of self, our martyrdom, whether "red" or "white." This is the path of self-emptying at the heart of the Christian story. This is the divine life flowing out from God and returning back to him, fulfilling in us the fundamental human vocation, revealed in Christ—to make a gift of ourselves in love. The self-mastery of the classical virtue tradition finds its perfection in the total self-giving love of Christian faith. As Wojtyła put it earlier, love fully actualizes the person. Love brings us to our true *telos*—happiness, union with God, and communion through total gift of self.

Redemptive Suffering

Our participation in the Paschal Mystery, Christ's death and Resurrection, has tremendous existential payoff, as we persevere in love to the very end (see John 13:1). For in and through our sufferings, *we can participate in the redemption of the world*.[18] What graces will be poured out—on us, our loved ones, and the world—because we united our sufferings to the Cross of Jesus Christ?

Plenty of suffering will eventually come our way, so there's no need to seek it out. Bearing suffering or misfortune (big or small) patiently and even with joy is one of the greatest gifts we can offer our loved ones. Indeed, our happiness—even when things aren't going our way—is often the greatest gift we can offer others. This is one of the hallmarks of the supernatural character of the Christian life, a tremendous testimony to its truth.

I close here with the words of my friend and colleague Matthew Ramage—who, in the midst of long bouts of immense suffering (including lupus, a kidney transplant, and the death of his father), found meaning through it all, precisely because of the distinctive Catholic teaching on redemptive suffering. This meaning became for him (and for so many) a powerful sign of the supernatural truth of the faith, even amid some of his darkest moments: "I have to ask myself: how could it be that the religion that produced such an immensely profound, fulfilling path of life be profoundly wrong in its most fundamental affirmations upon which its way of life is predicated?"[19]

Indeed, the *fruit* of the faith—manifest in these darkest of moments—points to the veracity of its *root*. The truth of Jesus redounds not only in the historical past but in the ever present—not least in its unrivaled power to offer meaning to those who suffer.

Although we have clearly already answered in the affirmative, we turn in our closing chapter to the question, *Does Christianity work?* Does it really make a difference in people's lives? And how do we account for the seemingly virtuous pagan among us? Or the scandal of Christians behaving badly?

I think you'll find Lewis's insights here penetrating and practical.

THIRTEEN
Does Christianity Really Work?

If Catholics have such riches at their disposal (especially in the Holy Eucharist), why aren't they, always and everywhere, burning with the joy of divine charity? Why aren't they, always and everywhere, just a bunch of walking saints?

The Scandal of the Sacraments

The mystery of the sacraments is twofold. On the one hand, they are *efficacious* signs, meaning they actually *effect* the grace they signify; they aren't mere symbols—they actually *do* something. This is the primary difference between the "signs" of the New Covenant (the sacraments) and their Old Covenant counterparts (e.g., circumcision, sacrifices). A common medieval contrast went like this:

Old Covenant Signs	New Covenant Signs
— Many	— Few
— Burdensome	— Easy
— Inefficacious (they symbolize grace but can't truly offer it)	— Efficacious (the Holy Spirit does what the sign symbolizes)[1]

This is the difference Christ makes.

And yet—on the other hand—as the *Catechism* makes clear, we receive the grace of the sacraments *in accordance with our faith and disposition* (see 1128). That is, the sacraments are not like a car wash; we are not mere passive recipients.

Consider the hemorrhaging woman in the gospels who touches the fringe of Jesus's garment and is healed. "Power" went forth from Christ, and her blood flow ceased. But when Jesus asks who touched him, Peter responds, "Master, the *multitudes* surround you and *press upon you!*" (Lk 8:45, emphasis added). *Many* touched Jesus—*just as many receive the sacraments*. But the woman touched in faith and was healed.

The sacraments are encounters with the risen Christ, as he continues to touch us and heal us in the present (see *CCC* 1116). The grace of the sacraments is always objectively on offer. But we receive this gift of divine life in accordance with our faith and disposition, to the extent that we approach with open hearts.

So, why aren't Catholics walking saints? Some, in fact, no doubt are. But many more would become so if our hearts were truly disposed to receive the sublime gift on offer.

You might be wondering, "But why don't I always *feel* the power of God in the sacraments?" Sometimes we do experience the presence and grace of God in the sacraments in a tangible way. But if this happened every time, we might return again and again just for the sake of this feeling. We would likely get addicted to this feeling and never come to love God for his own sake. In the sacramental encounter with our Lord, God wants us to grow in faith and love, and so in his providence the tangible feelings of his presence come and go. To love someone for how they make us feel is a start, but a tinge of selfishness remains. The full maturation of love occurs when we love another person for their own sake. God is always present to us, especially in the sacraments; but in his wisdom, he seeks to purify and mature our love. This is why we trust by the faith that far more is happening in the sacraments than we realize—here, we can't go by feelings alone.

Does Christianity Really Work?

Still, many wonder: *If Christianity is true, then why do we have the scandal of Christians sometimes behaving so badly?* And conversely: *Why do we sometimes see non-Christians living a more meaningful and virtuous life than their Christian counterparts?* For Lewis, to answer such questions, we need to compare each person against themselves. As he puts it: "If Christianity is true, then it ought to follow (a) That any Christian will be nicer *than the same person would be if he were not Christian*. (b) That any man who becomes a Christian will be nicer *than he was before.*"[2]

Or more pointedly: "*Christian* Miss Bates may have an unkinder tongue than *unbelieving* Dick Firkin. That, by itself, does not tell us whether Christianity works. The question is what Miss Bates's tongue would be like *if she were not a Christian* and what Dick's would be like *if he became one*."[3]

Speaking from my own experience, while there is some continuity in my pre- and post-conversion life (I have written elsewhere of my conversion experience in college),[4] there is also tremendous discontinuity. I have no doubt that—while not perfect—I quickly made moral and spiritual strides in my first years of truly becoming a Christian and embracing my Catholic faith, strides that I showed no signs of making prior. And by the grace of God (though not perfect), these moral and spiritual strides that began more than twenty years ago have only grown stronger ever since.

When I imagine how my life would have gone without my conversion, I see a relatively decent human being continuously searching for meaning in things that, while good—e.g., football, perhaps coaching, weightlifting, and working out—were never going to truly satisfy. I see someone who, while decent, never would have had the moral fiber or moral compass to truly find himself and lead a family someday.

Everything in my experience resonates deeply with Lewis's comments above. I became a better version of *myself* after giving my life to Christ. While my preconverted self "prefigures" my postconverted self in some ways, I never would have become what I am now if I had not given my life fully to Christ in the Catholic faith (though, like most of us, of course I still have a long way to go).

The Fear of Conversion

For many, the fear of conversion is the fear of "losing oneself." *If I go all in with Jesus, will I lose who I am? Will I become something I am not?* But as I and so many others can attest, when you give your life fully to Christ, you don't lose who you are—*you become a stronger, more enhanced version of who you've always been*. In the end, Christ takes the shallow, self-centered, and insecure part of us and gives us back so much more.[5]

To see this, Christianity must truly be *tried*. As G. K. Chesterton once said, "The Christian ideal has not been tried and found wanting. It has been found difficult; and *left untried*."[6] But what could be more worth our time and effort than giving our all here?

By all accounts, living the Christian life appears to help tremendously in living a better *natural* life. We might take this as an echo and indirect proof of its supernatural truth. Even more: What if supernatural life is around the corner, a divine life we can share in now and enjoy for all eternity? What if the "hero's journey" that Bilbo embodies is the path to which we're all called—and what if this path is far more than a universal human archetype, but the truth at the foundation of the cosmos, coming from the hand of a God who *is* love? It truly appears we have nothing to lose and everything to gain by giving our lives to Christ. With Bilbo, what is lost is the comfort of clinging to the familiar—what is lost is being a slave to fear. What is gained is our transformation and the finding of the very best version of ourselves on the far side of the journey.

To really experience the fruits of faith, one must be willing to take the risk of faith—one must take the journey. The truth of the Christian life is only seen (and felt) by sincerely living the Christian experiment, its truth becoming more manifest as we enter more fully into this way of life.[7] Those who do so are sure to taste its fruits; and our families and loved ones, no doubt, become the chief beneficiaries when we give our lives entirely over to Jesus.

So, what's holding you back?

Acknowledgments

I want to thank Ave Maria Press for supporting this project, and especially Kristi McDonald for her editorial work. Her support and input—both in terms of content and style—have been invaluable. Sincere thanks are also due to my very good friends, Dr. Matthew Ramage and Dr. James Madden, my colleagues at Benedictine College in theology and philosophy, respectively, who read advanced copies of the manuscript. Their shrewd analysis and willingness to press me with the questions of a skeptic greatly sharpened this work. I'm very grateful for their friendship. Of course, any infelicities that remain are solely my responsibility.

I wish also to thank the hundreds (and now thousands) of students I have taught over my eighteen years at Benedictine College. Passing on the Catholic intellectual tradition is a tremendous honor and joy. While it has been a great privilege to be part of their academic and spiritual formation, engaging their honest questions over the years has certainly formed me as well. In many ways, this book is the fruit of this ongoing dialogue.

Thanks especially to my beautiful bride, Sarah! There's nothing quite like publishing a book to mark our twentieth wedding anniversary! Thank you for journeying through life with me, through many twists and turns. I wouldn't be here without you!

And thanks also to our children, especially the older ones who helped shoulder the burden of my writing this book. I pray it bears fruit in their lives and that of many others.

Lastly, I give thanks to Almighty God; I stand in awe of his providence, especially when the closing of certain doors becomes the very means by which new ones open. Despite appearances to the contrary, God is always at work.

Historical Evidence for New Testament Figures Table by Lawrence Mykytiuk

The following table records the numerous figures from the New Testament who have been directly verified historically, either from material evidence archaeologically or from ancient historical sources of the period. This evidence illustrates how firmly the New Testament is rooted in the historical context of its day; it is a historical document, passing on the witness of people directly present at the time.

This table was originally published in Lawrence Mykytiuk, "30 People in the New Testament Confirmed," *Bible History Daily* (blog), September 7, 2017. Used by permission.

New Testament Figures Confirmed

Name	Who Were They?	When Did They Minister, Rule, or Flourish?
Religious Figures		
Jesus	Jewish preacher, healer, and teacher; called Christ; crucified by order of Pilate; then said to have risen.	c. 27–30 CE
Gamaliel the Elder	Renowned Pharisee who rescued the apostles.	c. 20–50 CE
John the Baptist	Jewish preacher of repentance; beheaded by Herod Antipas.	c. 26–29/30 CE
James	Jesus's relative; Jerusalem church leader; martyr.	c. 30–62 CE
Ananus/Annas	Son of Seth/Sethi; high priest and founder of a dynasty of high priests; first to interrogate Jesus.	High priest 6–15 CE
Caiaphas	High priest during Jesus's trial.	High priest 18–36/37 CE
Ananias	Son of Nebedaios, High priest at Paul's trial.	High priest 53–59 CE

by Historical Texts and Archaeology

Where in the New Testament?	Sample of Evidence in Historical Writings	Evidence in Inscriptions
All New Testament books except Third John but most often in the four gospels	Tacitus, Annals; Josephus, Antiquities; Lucian of Samosata, Passing of Peregrinus; Celsus, On the True Doctrine (via Origen, Against Celsus); Pliny the Younger, Epistulae	No inscribed monuments or coins
Acts 5:34–39; 22:3	Mishnah: Orlah; Rosh ha-Shanah; Yebamoth; Sotah; Gittin; Josephus, Life	No inscribed monuments or coins
Matthew 3:1–15; 11:2–18; Mark 1:1–9; 6:14–29; Luke 1:5–23; 7:18–33; John 1:6–8, 19–37; 3:23–34; Acts 1:5; 13:24–25; etc.	Josephus, *Antiquities*	No inscribed monuments or coins
Matthew 13:55; Mark 6.3; Acts 15:13; 21:18; Galatians 1:19; 2:9, 12	Josephus, *Antiquities*	No inscribed monuments or coins
Luke 3:2; John 18:13, 19–24; Acts 4:6	Josephus, *Antiquities*	No inscribed monuments or coins; Akeldama tomb potentially his.
Matthew 26:3, 57; Luke 3:2; John 11:49; 18:13–28; Acts 4:6	Josephus, *Antiquities*	No inscribed monuments or coins; inscribed ossuaries potentially name him.
Acts 25–26; 28:19	Josephus, *Antiquities*	No inscribed monuments or coins; Masada ostracon might name him.

New Testament Figures Confirmed

Name	Who Were They?	When Did They Minister, Rule, or Flourish?
Roman Emperors		
Augustus	Roman Emperor	31 BCE–14 CE
Tiberius	Roman Emperor	14–37 CE
Claudius	Roman Emperor	41–54 CE
Nero	Roman Emperor	54–68 CE
Herodian Family		
Herod I, the Great	Rome's King of the Jews over all of Palestine.	37–4 BCE
Herod Archelaus	Oldest son of Herod the Great. Ethnarch of Judea, Samaria, and Idumea.	4 BCE–6 CE
Herod Antipas	Son of Herod the Great; second husband of Herodias. Tetrarch of Galilee and Perea (Transjordan). He ordered the execution of John the Baptist.	4 BCE–39 CE
Herod Philip	Son of Herod the Great but not a ruler; Herodias's uncle and first husband; father of their daughter Salome.	
Herodias	Granddaughter of Herod the Great; niece and wife of Herod Philip, mother of his daughter Salome; then Herod Antipas's wife. She brought about the order to execute John the Baptist.	

by Historical Texts and Archaeology continued

Where in the New Testament?	Sample of Evidence in Historical Writings	Evidence in Inscriptions
Luke 2:1	Numerous	Numerous
Luke 3:1	Numerous	Numerous
Acts 11:28; 18:2	Numerous	Numerous
Acts 25–26; 28:19	Numerous	Numerous
Matthew 2:1; Luke 1:5	Josephus, *Antiquities* and *Wars*	Coins
Matthew 2:22	Josephus, *Antiquities* and *Wars*	Coins
Luke 3:1; 13:31–32; 23:7–12; Mark 6:14; 6:16–28; 8:15	Josephus, *Antiquities* and *Wars*	Coins
Matthew 14:3–4; Mark 6:17–18; Luke 3:19	Josephus, *Antiquities* and *Wars*	(No coins because he was not a ruler)
Matthew 14:2–11; Mark 6:17–28; Luke 3:19–20	Josephus, *Antiquities* and *Wars*	(No coins because she was not a ruler)

New Testament Figures Confirmed

Name	Who Were They?	When Did They Minister, Rule, or Flourish?
Herodian Family continued		
Salome	Herodias's daughter. Her dance led to the execution of John the Baptist. Grandniece and later wife of Philip the Tetrarch.	
Philip the Tetrarch	Son of Herod the Great. Tetrarch of Trachonitis, Iturea, and other northern portions of Palestine. Eventually husband of his grandniece Salome.	4 BCE–34 CE
Herod Agrippa I	Grandson of Herod the Great; brother of Herodias. King of Trachonitis, Batanea, gradually all of Palestine. Executed James the son of Zebedee and imprisoned Peter.	37–44 CE
Herod Agrippa II	Son of Herod Agrippa I. Initially Tetrarch of Iturea and Trachonitis, then also over parts of Galilee and Perea, Chalcis and northern territories. Festus appointed him to hear Paul's defense.	50–c. 93 CE
Berenice/Bernice	Sister and companion of Herod Agrippa II, rumored lovers. Attended Paul's trial before Festus.	
Drusilla	Sister of Herodias and Herod Agrippa I, Jewish wife of Roman governor Felix.	

by Historical Texts and Archaeology continued

Where in the New Testament?	Sample of Evidence in Historical Writings	Evidence in Inscriptions
Matthew 14:3–12; Mark 6:17–29	Josephus, *Antiquities*	Coins of her husband, Aristobulus, king of Chalcis
Luke 3:1	Josephus, *Antiquities* and *Wars*	Coins
Acts 12:1–6, 18–23	Josephus, *Antiquities* and *Wars*	Coins
Acts 25:13–26:32	Josephus, *Antiquities* and *Wars*	Coins
Acts 25:13, 23; 26:30	Josephus, *Antiquities* and *Wars*	Inscription of King Herod Agrippa II in Beirut
Acts 24:24	Josephus, *Antiquities*	(No coins because she was not a ruler)

New Testament Figures Confirmed

Name	Who Were They?	When Did They Minister, Rule, or Flourish?
Roman Legate and Governors		
Publius Sulpicius Quirinius (=Cyrenius)	Roman imperial legate brought in to govern Syria-Cilicia after Herod Archelaus's rule led to rebellion.	6–9 CE and possibly earlier
Pontius Pilate	Roman prefect of Judea who conducted Jesus's trial and ordered his crucifixion.	26–36 CE
Lucius Junius Gallio	Roman proconsul of Achaia who convened and dismissed the trial of Paul in Corinth.	c. 51–55 CE
Marcus Antonius Felix	Roman procurator of Judea who held initial hearings in the trial of the apostle Paul.	52–c. 59 CE
Porcius Festus	Roman procurator of Judea who conducted a hearing in the trial of Paul, during which Paul appealed to Caesar and was sent to Rome.	59–62 CE
Independent Political Figures		
Aretas IV	Arabian king of Nabatea. Father of Herod Antipas's first wife, before Herodias.	9 BCE–40 CE
The unnamed Egyptian leader	His Jerusalem-area insurrection was suppressed by Roman procurator Felix.	
Judas of Galilee	Led a rebellion against the census of Roman imperial legate Quirinius.	

by Historical Texts and Archaeology continued

Where in the New Testament?	Sample of Evidence in Historical Writings	Evidence in Inscriptions
Luke 2:2	Josephus, *Antiquities* and *Wars*	The Lapis Venetus inscription discovered in Beirut
Matthew 27:11–26; Mark 15:1–15; Luke 3:1; 23:1–24; John 18:28–19:22	Josephus, *Antiquities* and *Wars*; Tacitus, *Annals*; Philo, *De Legatione ad Gaium*	Pilate stone discovered at Caesarea Maritima; coins
Acts 18:12–17	Seneca, *Letters*; Tacitus, *Annals*	Stone inscription discovered in Delphi, Greece
Acts 23; 24	Josephus, *Antiquities* and *Wars*	Coins
Acts 24:27–25:27; 26:24–32	Josephus, *Antiquities*	Coins
2 Corinthians 11:32	Josephus, *Antiquities* and *Wars*	Inscription at Petra, etc.; coins
Acts 21:38	Josephus, *Antiquities* and *Wars*	(No coins because he was not a ruler)
Acts 5:37	Josephus, *Antiquities* and *Wars*	(No coins because he was not a ruler)

Notes

Introduction

1. "Catholic" is a combination of two Greek words (*kata* + *holos*) and literally means "according to the whole."
2. See George Sayer, *Jack: A Life of C. S. Lewis* (Wheaton, IL: Crossway, 1988), 421–22.
3. However, in recent years, we have also seen non-Catholic Christians show a deeper desire for a more embodied liturgical and sacramental experience, sometimes exhibiting a sincere openness to the liturgical practice of the early Church. Anecdotally, I saw this already in my time at Trinity Evangelical Divinity School from 2004 to 2006 (where I received a master's degree in Old Testament & Semitic Languages and was affectionately known as "Catholic Andy"). More recently, at a jiu-jitsu tournament in Florida in 2023, my wife and I had a long conversation with a nondenominational Protestant, whose pastor had introduced his congregation to the ancient practice of Lent—and he was loving it!
4. St. Augustine, *Confessions*, trans. R. S. Pine-Coffin (New York: Penguin, 1961), 108.

1. What Is a Human? and Why the Question of Humanity Matters

1. See *Gaudium et Spes* 36 and *Evangelium Vitae* 22.
2. C. S. Lewis, *Mere Christianity* (San Francisco: HarperCollins, 2001), 3.
3. Ibid.
4. Ibid.
5. Ibid., 4, emphasis added.
6. This point is more likely (or possibly) true when looking at stars only visible through a telescope, because of their greater distance from us.
7. See Mortimer J. Adler, *How to Think About the Great Ideas: From the Great Books of Western Civilization*, ed. Max Weismann (Chicago: Open Court, 2000), 82.
8. See Ric Machuga, *In Defense of the Soul: What It Means to Be Human* (Grand Rapids, MI: Brazos, 2002), 111–17, 157. See also Mortimer J. Adler, *Intellect: Mind over Matter* (New York: Macmillan, 1990), 34.
9. Ibid., 78.
10. See James D. Madden, *Thinking About Thinking: Mind and Meaning in the Era of Techno-Nihilism* (Eugene, OR: Cascade, 2023), 103–6.
11. See Peter Kreeft, *Socratic Logic: A Logic Text Using Socratic Method, Platonic Questions, and Aristotelian Principles*, 3rd ed. (South Bend, IN: St. Augustine's Press, 2008), 35–46.

12. Adler, *Intellect: Mind over Matter*, 63. Or perhaps one can say that what we mean by "knowledge" is something accruing to a *biological organism*, as it learns to interact with its environment and understand its most fundamental causes (making human "knowledge" different from AI). See William A. Wallace, *The Elements of Philosophy: A Compendium for Philosophers and Theologians* (New York: Alba House, 1977), 111.

13. See *Nicomachean Ethics*, 1.13, cited from *Aristotle: Nicomachean Ethics*, 2nd ed., trans. Terence Irwin (Indianapolis, IN: Hackett, 1999), 17.

14. Cited in Madden, *Thinking About Thinking*, 147, emphasis added. For Haugeland, human "care" actually grounds our reason. I thank James Madden for this insight.

15. Ibid., 155, emphasis added.

2. The Fulfillment of All Desire

1. See Stephen M. Barr, *Modern Physics and Ancient Faith* (Notre Dame, IN: University of Notre Dame Press, 2003), 43–52. Other scenarios, which suppose that the Big Bang was not truly the beginning of the cosmos, still point to the contingency of the cosmos—because we clearly have a *changing* cosmos (not a static cosmos). And in our experience, what exhibits change is contingent.

2. See Mortimer J. Adler, *How to Think About God: A Guide for the 20th-Century Pagan* (New York: Macmillan, 1980), 144: "Whatever can be otherwise than it is can also simply not be at all. A cosmos which can *be otherwise* is one that also can *not be*. . . . A merely possible cosmos cannot be an uncaused cosmos" (emphasis in original). See also Andrew Dean Swafford, *John Paul II to Aristotle and Back Again: A Christian Philosophy of Life* (Eugene, OR: Wipf and Stock, 2015), 8–12. Our best examples of necessary truths tend to be logical and mathematical truths ("all bachelors are unmarried" or "two plus two equals four"). If the universe ceased to exist (as long as there was a mind to consider the proposition), these two statements would remain true and perennially valid. But is the *existence* of the universe like one of these *logical* truths that transcends the material order? It would seem not. The existence of the universe demands an explanation, one that transcends the physical, changing, temporal universe.

3. See Anthony Rizzi, *The Science Before Science: A Guide to Thinking in the 21st Century* (Baton Rouge, LA: Institute for Advanced Physics, 2004), 266. The worry of Immanuel Kant (1724–1804) is that though this reasoning may be sound, it reflects the fundamental structures of the human mind—not the way things really are. While Kant is not wrong to express this worry, the fundamental posture of the Christian is that our knowing faculties truly put us in touch with reality. It is an existential posture of trust—that there truly is a ladder from the way things appear to the way things really are.

4. Barr, *Modern Physics and Ancient Faith*, 80.

5. Cardinal Schönborn helpfully distinguishes between "evolution" (as a scientific theory) and "evolutionism" (as a materialistic philosophy). A Catholic can accept the former, but not the latter. See Christoph Cardinal Schönborn, *Chance or Purpose: Creation, Evolution, and a Rational Faith*, trans. Henry Taylor (San Francisco: Ignatius Press, 2007), 22–31, 115, 123, 167–69.

6. Antony Flew, *There Is a God: How the World's Most Notorious Atheist Changed His Mind* (New York: HarperCollins, 2007), 110, 112.

7. See Swafford, *John Paul II to Aristotle and Back Again*, 2–8, and Barr, *Modern Physics and Ancient Faith*, 76–112. In a more nuanced direction, a very precise order seems to be present at the opening moments of the Big Bang, such that if things were off ever so slightly, the eventual development of life would have been impossible. Examples include the strength of the strong nuclear force, the process by which carbon is formed, and the strength of the electromagnetic force (see Barr, *Modern Physics and Ancient Faith*, 119–26; Stephen C. Meyer, *Return of the God Hypothesis: Three Scientific Discoveries That Reveal the Mind Behind the Universe* [New York: HarperOne, 2021], 146–60; Geraint F. Lewis and Luke A. Barnes, *A Fortunate Universe: Life in a Finely Tuned Cosmos* [Cambridge, UK: Cambridge University Press, 2016]; and Robert J. Spitzer, *New Proofs for the Existence of God: Contributions of Contemporary Physics and Philosophy* [Grand Rapids, MI: Eerdmans, 2010], 47–74). In the words of Antony Flew, the atheist-turned-theist, it looks like "*someone knew you were coming*" (*There Is a God*, 114). Flew suggests that it would be like showing up at a hotel room, only to see your favorite book by your favorite author opened to your favorite chapter on the table, and then turning to see your favorite painting on the wall and your favorite beverage in the refrigerator. Then you notice that your favorite song is playing. With each successive occurrence, the conviction becomes ever clearer: *Somebody prepared the room especially for you because they knew you were coming* (see ibid., 113–16). As Flew and other thinkers argue, the fine-tuning of the fundamental constants of our universe seems especially designed to make life on our planet possible—*it seems as if someone knew we were coming*.

8. This, again, is not to speak for or against evolution as a scientific theory. We can see design in the fundamental order of the cosmos, in the environment that culls forth certain traits, and in the individual organism itself. As a scientific theory, evolution answers a *how* question (how did things develop?), not the ultimate question (where did it all come from?).

9. See the Regensberg address, given by Pope Benedict in September of 2006: https://www.cbcew.org.uk/full-text-of-the-pope-benedict-xvis-regensburg-lecture/.

10. For a deeper explanation as to why these arguments from contingency and design pose no threat whatsoever to the practice of science, see Swafford, *John Paul II to Aristotle and Back Again*, 2–12.

11. See Jean-Paul Sartre, *Existentialism Is a Humanism*, cited in *Existentialism*, ed. Robert C. Solomon (New York: Random House, 1974), 201–2.
12. Lewis, *Mere Christianity*, 135–36.
13. Ibid., emphasis added.
14. Ibid., 136.
15. Ibid.
16. Ibid., 137, emphasis added.
17. Ibid., emphasis added.
18. *The Confessions: Saint Augustine of Hippo*, trans. Maria Boulding (San Francisco: Ignatius Press, 2012), 3.
19. See John Henry Newman, *A Letter Addressed to the Duke of Norfolk: On Occasion of Mr. Gladstone's Recent Expostulation* (New York: Aeterna, 2015), 41–42.
20. Lewis, *Mere Christianity*, 29.
21. Ibid., 30.
22. See Edward T. Oakes, "Newman's Liberal Problem," *First Things* 132 (2003).
23. See Carl R. Trueman, *The Rise and Triumph of the Modern Self* (Wheaton, IL: Crossway, 2020).
24. It is remarkable how many people attest—especially in private anonymous surveys—to having had religious experiences of some sort with God or the transcendent, even people who claim to be atheists. See Dale C. Allison Jr., *Encountering Mystery: Religious Experience in a Secular Age* (Grand Rapids, MI: Eerdmans, 2022), 9, 21. Intriguingly, Allison notes that pastors and theologians seem *uninterested* and skeptical of these experiences that people so often claim to have had (see ibid., 10–11). This is clearly a mistake, as encountering the divine is often a crucial moment for people in their journey of faith.
25. Philosophically, this is known as "scientism."
26. Alex Rosenberg, *The Atheist's Guide to Reality: Enjoying Life Without Illusions* (New York: W. W. Norton & Co., 2011), 96. Similarly, Rosenberg writes: "Nihilism can't condemn Hitler, Stalin, Mao, Pol Pot, or those who fomented the Armenian genocide or the Rwandan one. If there is no such thing as 'morally forbidden,' then what Mohamed Atta did on September 11, 2001, was not morally forbidden" (ibid., 98).
27. See Joseph Ratzinger, *Introduction to Christianity*, trans. J. R. Foster (San Francisco: Ignatius Press, 1990), 43.

3. I Want to Be Happy—So Why Should I Care About Morality?

1. See *Gaudium et Spes* 22.
2. Lewis, *Mere Christianity*, 69.
3. See Alasdair MacIntyre, *After Virtue*, 2nd ed. (Notre Dame, IN: University of Notre Dame Press, 1984), 52.

4. Potency is an exceedingly important concept when it comes to life issues, as I have articulated elsewhere: "The pro-life position is based on the view that when the life of the new human organism begins, the person comes into existence. Interestingly, it's often the pro-choice side—at least in academic circles—that avoids the question as to when the human organism begins and focuses more on questions of 'personhood,' often opting to frame personhood (which is when they take moral and legal rights to begin) in terms of self-consciousness and awareness. But such a view of 'personhood' is very slippery—after all, how 'self-conscious' is a three-month-old? What we want is to 'divide nature at its joints,' as it were, and to do so we need to look at the nature of things—how they act and react. A sperm left to itself will never become a mature human being. But a newly conceived embryo has everything it needs internally to self-develop into a mature human being. This radical difference in potency (or self-developing capacity) between a sperm and a newly conceived embryo is enough to note a radical difference in nature between the two. Therefore, the sperm is a *potential human being*—say, if it were to later join with an ovum; but an embryo is a *human being with potential*" (Swafford, *John Paul II to Aristotle and Back Again*, 17, no. 5).

5. See Michael Allen Gillespie, *Nihilism Before Nietzsche* (Chicago: University of Chicago Press, 1995), 14–28, and *Ockham: Philosophical Writings*, ed. and trans. Philotheus Boehner, rev. Stephen F. Brown (Indianapolis, IN: Hackett, 1990), xxvii.

6. This is certainly not to say that all "modern" developments are necessarily bad. Certainly the "personalism" of St. John Paul II is inspired in part by developments in modern philosophy.

7. We should note that there are different forms of nominalism, some more extreme than others. What we are concerned with here is the overall framework in which one views and lives out the moral life and how the turn toward nominalism in the fourteenth century affects this overall perspective.

8. It's also the case that nominalism cynically disconnects our language (and commonsense perception of the world) from the real. We're not far from seeing human speech (and our attempts at making truth claims) as nothing more than a language game and assertion of power.

9. See the *Euthyphro*, 10d, cited in *Plato: Five Dialogues*, 2nd ed., trans. G. M. A. Grube (Indianapolis, IN: Hackett, 2002), 13.

10. See Servais Pinckaers, *The Sources of Christian Ethics*, trans. Mary Thomas Noble (Washington, DC: Catholic University of America Press, 1995), 240–53. See also Gillespie, *Nihilism Before Nietzsche*, 21–22, and Louis Dupré, *Passage to Modernity: An Essay in the Hermeneutics of Nature and Culture* (New Haven, CT: Yale University Press, 1993), 120–44, as well as Brad S. Gregory, *The Unintended Reformation: How a Religious Revolution Secularized Society* (Cambridge, MA: Harvard University Press, 2012), 180–234.

11. *ST* I q. 4, a. 1: "All created perfections are in God."

12. There are hard cases, such as when it appears that God commands the prophet Hosea to marry a prostitute (see Hosea 1:2–3).

13. For what it's worth, in the three options above, one can see a common dynamic at work in the history of the Church. The voluntarist view is simple and straightforward—goodness flows from what God decides, and God can do whatever he wants. In general, heresy tends to represent a simpler, more straightforward option; very often, the heretic is resistant to paradox and mystery and seeks to simplify and truncate the mystery. See Andrew Dean Swafford, *Nature and Grace: A New Approach to Thomistic Ressourcement* (Eugene, OR: Pickwick, 2014), 52.

14. See John Paul II, *Crossing the Threshold of Hope*, ed. Vittorio Messori (New York: Alfred A. Knopf, 2016), 228: "Original sin attempts . . . to abolish fatherhood, destroying its rays which permeate the created world, placing in doubt the truth about God who is Love and leaving man only with a sense of the master-slave relationship. As a result, the Lord appears jealous of His power over the world and over man; and consequently, man feels goaded to do battle against God."

15. This type of freedom will be developed more fully in the next chapter.

16. Karol Wojtyła, *Love and Responsibility*, trans. Grzegorz Ignatik (Boston, MA: Pauline Press, 2013), 117.

4. Freedom and Virtue

1. This seems in part because we are far more concerned with politics than ethics (that is, the kind of people we are becoming).

2. See Andrew and Sarah Swafford, *Gift and Grit: How Heroic Virtue Can Change Your Life and Relationships* (West Chester, PA: Ascension Press, 2023), 38–42.

3. Lewis, *Mere Christianity*, 71.

4. Ibid.

5. Ibid., 74.

6. See *Nicomachean Ethics*, 10.7, cited from *Aristotle: Nicomachean Ethics*, 163–65.

7. See Alasdair MacIntyre, *After Virtue: A Study in Moral Theory*, 2nd ed. (Notre Dame, IN: University of Notre Dame Press, 1984), 122–23, 135–36; *Nicomachean Ethics*, books 8 and 9.

8. For Karol Wojtyła (later John Paul II), *love* fully actualizes our nature: "Love ... most fully develops the existence of the person" (*Love and Responsibility*, trans. Grzegorz Ignatik [Boston, MA: Pauline, 2013], 66; see also ibid., 80).

9. *Confessions* 2.1, cited in *The Confessions*, trans. Boulding, 33, emphasis added.

10. Swafford, *John Paul II to Aristotle and Back Again*, 28–29.

11. Ibid., 29–30.
12. *Nicomachean Ethics* 2.3, cited in *Aristotle: Nicomachean Ethics*, 20.
13. Lewis, *Mere Christianity*, 192.
14. See Sarah Swafford, *Emotional Virtue: A Guide to Drama-Free Relationships* (Denver, CO: Totus Tuus, 2014), 49–60.

5. What Are the Virtues?

1. Lewis, *Mere Christianity*, 78, emphasis added.
2. *Nicomachean Ethics* 2.6, cited in *Aristotle: Nicomachean Ethics*, 25.
3. *Nicomachean Ethics* 3.11.7, cited in *Aristotle: Nicomachean Ethics*, 47.
4. *Confessions* 5.10, cited in *The Confessions*, trans. Boulding, 119.
5. See Abigail Favale, *The Genesis of Gender: A Christian Theory* (San Francisco: Ignatius Press, 2022), 199–200. This dualistic thinking also underlies transgender ideology. While there are certainly persons who suffer from gender dysphoria and need to be treated with compassion, as an ideology, transgenderism—like ancient Gnosticism—assumes that the real self is somehow separate from the body (and can, therefore, be "trapped" in the "wrong" body). But when we see the unity of the human person as a body-soul composite, then we can say that *the body is essential and constitutive of who and what I am*. In a deep way, *I am my body*. The same issue occurs with abortion. Many pro-abortion academics acknowledge that the individual human being is present at conception but insist that the individual human organism is not yet a "person." They identify personhood (as the seat of moral and legal rights) with consciousness, self-awareness, and the like. In contrast, the pro-life position insists that when the individual human organism is present, the *person* is present—because, once again, I am a body-soul composite; *I* am not separate from my body (see Patrick Lee, "The Prolife Argument from Substantial Identity," *Bioethics* 18 [2004]: 249–63).
6. See Wojtyła, *Love and Responsibility*, 42–45.
7. *ST* I-IIae q. 94.
8. Wojtyła employs a concept derived from St. Augustine under the Latin term *frui*, which means the joy, delight, or pleasure that accompanies a rightly ordered action. If the action is rightly ordered, this *frui* is positively good and divinely ordained. See *Love and Responsibility*, 45.
9. Ibid.
10. Josef Pieper, *The Four Cardinal Virtues* (Notre Dame, IN: University of Notre Dame Press, 1966), 147–48.
11. Wojtyła accepts the traditional view of chastity as a subset of temperance, but he wishes to go further: For him, the full sense of chastity can only be understood in connection with the virtue of love. Chastity liberates our love from the attitude of "to use" and frees us to love the other for their own sake, not merely for what they can do for us. See *Love and Responsibility*, 154–55.

12. See Lewis, *Mere Christianity*, 79, and Andrew and Sarah Swafford, *Gift and Grit*, 46–48.
13. See *ST* II-IIae q. 136, a. 1, 4.
14. See Brant Pitre, *Introduction to the Spiritual Life: Walking the Path of Prayer with Jesus* (New York: Image, 2021), 185–86.
15. *ST* II-IIae q. 81, a. 3, 5 ad 3.
16. See Scott Hahn and Brandon McGinley, *It Is Right and Just: Why the Future of Civilization Depends on True Religion* (Steubenville, OH: Emmaus, 2020).
17. *ST* II-IIae q. 47, a. 4.
18. As Wojtyła describes, there's always some battle—some pain involved—at the meeting point between "freedom" and the "sexual drive." As a person, we have an interiority that is rational and free—we have the ability of self-determination. And yet, we also experience our sexual drive spontaneously. See *Love and Responsibility*, 30, 117–18.
19. See Gregory K. Popcak, *Holy Sex! A Catholic Guide to Toe-Curling, Mind-Blowing, Infallible Loving* (New York: Crossroad, 2008), 164.
20. Lewis, *Mere Christianity*, 79.
21. C. S. Lewis, *The Screwtape Letters* (New York: HarperCollins, 2001), 161–62, emphasis added.
22. Lewis, *Mere Christianity*, 80.
23. Ibid.
24. Ibid.
25. Ibid., 81.
26. Ibid., 81. Fulton Sheen makes a similar observation: "If [the soul] sees itself irremediably vitiated, having no likeness whatever to the purity and holiness of God; if it has lost all affection for the things of the spirit, then it could no more endure the presence of God than a man who abhors beauty could endure the pleasure of music, art, and poetry. *Why, heaven would be hell to such a soul*, for it would be as much out of place in the holiness of heaven as a fish out of water" (*God to Heaven: A Spiritual Road Map to Eternity* [San Francisco: Ignatius Press, 2017], 229, emphasis added).
27. These virtues are called "cardinal" based on the Latin word *cardo*, meaning "hinge"; thus these are the virtues upon a which human life "hinges."
28. *Redemptor Hominis* 1.

6. Who Is Jesus, and How Can We Be Sure?

1. Jaroslav Pelikan, *The Christian Tradition: A History of the Development of Doctrine*, vol. 1, *The Emergence of the Catholic Tradition (100–600)* (Chicago: University of Chicago Press, 1971), 63. This more directly concerns the Platonic tradition, but our treatment of Aristotle exemplifies an important aspect

of what originates with Socrates and Plato (since Aristotle was Plato's student), namely, the central importance of virtue in the good life.

2. Lewis, *Mere Christianity*, 50.

3. See Louis Markos, *The Myth Made Fact: Reading Greek and Roman Mythology Through Christian Eyes* (Camp Hill, PA: Classical Academic, 2020).

4. The Church Fathers distinguish between *theologia* and *oikonomia*, Greek words referring respectively to *who* God is and *what he does* in time and history to father his family (see *CCC* 236). All of theology, the study of God's revelation, revolves around these two poles—who God is as Triune, and what he does for us in salvation history (including the sacraments).

5. This is quoting the Septuagint, the Greek Old Testament, often abbreviated as "LXX," on account of the tradition of seventy Jewish translators behind this ancient version of the Old Testament.

6. Lewis, *Mere Christianity*, 51–52.

7. Ibid., 52.

8. Bart D. Ehrman, *How Jesus Became God: The Exaltation of a Jewish Preacher from Galilee* (New York: HarperCollins, 2014), 124–28. Ehrman sees the following passages as clear examples of Jesus's divine identity in the Gospel of John: 8:58; 10:30; 14:9; 17:24 (see ibid., 124). This is noteworthy. For Ehrman, Jesus's divinity was certainly not "invented" at the Council of Nicaea by Constantine but is clearly present centuries before, albeit (in his view) a teaching not going back to the historical Jesus himself.

9. Craig S. Keener, *The Historical Jesus of the Gospels* (Grand Rapids, MI: Eerdmans, 2009), 78–80.

10. Brant Pitre, *The Case for Jesus: The Biblical and Historical Evidence for Christ* (New York: Image, 2016), 71–75.

11. Keener, *The Historical Jesus of the Gospels*, 96–98, 123–25.

12. While in the modern context, we can easily imagine hypothetical examples (say, in twentieth-century communism) where wholesale lies are made up about a revolutionary leader purely for propaganda purposes—this is just not how the ancient genre of Greco-Roman biography worked. While these ancient biographies were certainly written from a particular perspective and aimed to portray a person in a particular light, the portrayal was understood to have limits; it wasn't acceptable to simply make things up. As an example of how biblical history works (including the gospels), consider someone painting a tree outside: The painting is *not* the tree because the painting embodies the artist's creative portrayal of the tree. And yet the artist's creativity is constrained by the real—by the external reality of the tree that he or she is painting (that is, the artist's creativity is not unlimited). Similarly, biblical history does have a creative dimension, in terms of how the author portrays a particular event and the meaning the author seeks to draw out. And yet—like the artist—the biblical historian's creativity is constrained by the external reality, namely, the events themselves. See V. Philips Long, *The Art*

of Biblical History (Grand Rapids, MI: Zondervan Academic, 1994). Further, in the context of the gospels, we have not one biography, but *four*. Against the backdrop of the genre of ancient Greco-Roman biography—especially with four separate biographies—there is no reason to think the gospel writers are simply "making things up" in the manner of the hypothetical communist example above.

13. Cited in Pitre, *The Case for Jesus*, 82, emphasis added.
14. Ehrman, *How Jesus Became God*, 172.
15. See Pitre, *The Case for Jesus*, 86–87.
16. See Dale Allison, *Constructing Jesus: Memory, Imagination, and History* (Grand Rapids, MI: Baker Academic, 2010), 13, 24. We also have ancient accounts of students taking notes of their master's teaching (Keener, *The Historical Jesus of the Gospels*, 148–49). It's quite possible this occurred, especially with someone like Matthew, a tax collector, whose profession would most likely imply his literacy (Pitre, *The Case for Jesus*, 27).
17. Keener, *The Historical Jesus of the Gospels*, 146. See also Allison, *Constructing Jesus*, 29.
18. See Yves Congar, *Tradition and Traditions: The Biblical, Historical, and Theological Evidence for Catholic Teaching on Tradition* (New York: Simon and Schuster, 1966), 354.
19. See Pitre, *The Case for Jesus*, 16, 39–52.
20. *Against Heresies* 3.1, cited in Pitre, *The Case for Jesus*, 41.
21. See ibid., 39–51.
22. See ibid., 27.
23. Luke, of course, is unique in that his mentor (St. Paul) did not know Jesus in Jesus's earthly life. However, Luke implies that he interviewed eyewitnesses to write his gospel: "Inasmuch as many have undertaken to compile a narrative of the things which have been accomplished among us, *just as they were delivered to us by those who from the beginning were eyewitnesses* and ministers of the word, it seemed good to me also, having followed all things closely for some time past, to write an orderly account for you, most excellent Theophilus, that you may know the truth concerning the things of which you have been informed" (Lk 1:1–4).
24. See Pitre, *The Case for Jesus*, 22–23.
25. See Ehrman, *How Jesus Became God*, 90.
26. See Pitre, *The Case for Jesus*, 61–62.
27. See Mark Goodacre, *Thomas and the Gospels: The Case for Thomas's Familiarity with the Synoptics* (Grand Rapids, MI: Eerdmans, 2012), 154–92, and Darrell L. Bock, *Breaking the Da Vinci Code* (Nashville, TN: Nelson, 2004), 61–98.
28. See Craig A. Evans, *Jesus and His World: The Archaeological Evidence* (Louisville, KY: Westminster John Knox, 2012), 9–10. See also the chart from the 2017 (September/October) edition of *Biblical Archaeology Review*:

https://www.biblicalarchaeology.org/daily/people-cultures-in-the-bible/people-in-the-bible/new-testament-political-figures-the-evidence/#end01.

29. This is a point in favor of the historicity of the canonical gospels, since the move to de-Judaize Jesus (say, in the Gnostic texts) is actually quite foreign to the Jesus of history; as virtually every historical Jesus scholar assumes, the historical Jesus must be firmly rooted in his first-century Jewish context. Any pretensions to a *non-Jewish* Jesus are simply made up.

30. Richard Bauckham, *Jesus and the Eyewitnesses: The Gospel as Eyewitness Testimony* (Grand Rapids, MI: Eerdmans, 2006), 490–508.

31. See Jonathan Bernier, *Rethinking the Dates of the New Testament: The Evidence for Early Composition* (Grand Rapids, MI: Baker Academic, 2022), 38–84, and Pitre, *The Case for Jesus*, 89–94, 98–101.

32. Pitre, *The Case for Jesus*, 98–101.

33. See Bernier, *Rethinking the Dates of the New Testament*, 82–83.

34. See Pitre, *The Case for Jesus*, 92, and *Early Judaism: A Comprehensive Overview*, ed. John J. Collins and Daniel C. Harlow (Grand Rapids, MI: Eerdmans, 2012), 59.

35. Peter Kreeft and Ronald K. Tacelli, *Handbook of Christian Apologetics: Hundreds of Answers to Crucial Questions* (Downers Grove, IL: IVP Academic, 1994), 163.

36. See Babylonian Talmud, *Sanhedrin* 43a. However, some dispute that the "Yeshu" who is described as being executed actually refers to Jesus of Nazareth (see Brant Pitre, *Jesus and the Last Supper* [Grand Rapids, MI: Eerdmans, 2015], 292–95).

37. Although this is an argument from silence (and therefore not demonstrative), it is still worth noting.

38. Our claims here are about what is "reasonable." There's always an element of trust. Just as we trust that our knowing faculties put us in touch with the real (as we move from the contingency of creation to the Creator, or from the voice of conscience to the Voice of the Creator), so, too, here we need a fundamental posture of trust—that the witness of Jesus's followers truly puts us in touch with the Lord Jesus himself. This trust is eminently reasonable at the level of historical reasoning. But it is still trust in the testimony of Jesus's disciples and the ecclesial community he left us.

7. The Divinity of Jesus

1. *The Confessions*, trans. Boulding, 127.

2. *Saint Augustine: Confessions*, trans. R. S. Pine-Coffin, 108, emphasis added.

3. Lewis, *The Screwtape Letters*, 39.

4. See Michael Patrick Barber, *The Historical Jesus and the Temple: Memory, Methodology, and the Gospel of Matthew* (Cambridge, UK: Cambridge University Press, 2023), 20–42.

5. Ibid., 26–27.

6. Ibid., emphasis in original.

7. I am drawing from Brant Pitre's triple-context approach to the historical Jesus (which he himself has modified from E. P. Sanders): *contextual plausibility, coherence with other evidence about Jesus*, and *plausibility of effects in early Christianity*. See Pitre, *Jesus and the Last Supper*, 34–46. To describe the third aspect (plausibility of effects in early Christianity), Pitre frequently uses phrasing such as "plausible point of origin." See Brant Pitre, *Jesus and Divine Christology* (Grand Rapids, MI: Eerdmans, 2024), 63, 125, 144–45, 165, 215, 321.

8. For example, the Dead Sea Scrolls speak of a "messiah of Israel" to refer to a royal Davidic Messiah, and a "messiah of Aaron" to refer to a priestly Messiah. See the *Rule of the Congregration* 1Q281 and the *Damascus Document* 4Q266, cited respectively in *The Dead Sea Scrolls: Study Edition*, vol. 1, ed. Florentino García Martínez and Eibert J. C. Tigchelaar (Grand Rapids, MI: Eerdmans, 1997), 103, 571, 575. See also John J. Collins, *The Scepter and the Star: Messianism in Light of the Dead Sea Scrolls*, 2nd ed. (Grand Rapids, MI: Eerdmans, 2010), 79–109.

9. However, there are some Jewish apocalyptic traditions that speak of a hidden and seemingly preexistent (quasi-divine) Messiah. See Brant Pitre, Michael P. Barber, and John A. Kincaid, *Paul, a New Covenant Jew: Rethinking Pauline Theology* (Grand Rapids, MI: Eerdmans, 2019), 88–90.

10. Pitre, *The Case for Jesus*, 159–61. See also Matthew J. Ramage, *Jesus, Interpreted: Benedict XVI, Bart Ehrman, and the Historical Truth of the Gospels* (Washington, DC: Catholic University of America Press, 2017), 128.

11. Translation mine.

12. *Letter to the Ephesians*, ch. 7, cited in *Ignatius of Antioch and Polycarp: A New Translation and Theological Commentary*, trans. Kenneth J. Howell (Zanesville, OH: CHResources, 2009), 80, emphasis added.

13. See Pitre, *Jesus and Divine Christology*, 109–68.

14. Translation mine. While *ego eimi* can be simply a way of identifying oneself (see John 9:9), contextual clues here make it clear that the divine name is in view here. See Pitre, *Jesus and Divine Christology*, 71–75.

15. See Pitre, *The Case for Jesus*, 119–54, and Pitre, *Jesus and Divine Christology*, 40–245. Not least is the Transfiguration scene found in all three Synoptic Gospels (see Matthew 17:1–9; Mark 9:2–10; and Luke 9:28–36).

8. The Resurrection of Jesus

1. Ehrman, *How Jesus Became God*, 146, emphasis added.

2. Ibid., 143.
3. Ibid., 163–64.
4. *De Iosepho* 22–23, cited in Craig A. Evans and N. T. Wright, *Jesus, the Final Days: What Really Happened*, ed. Troy Miller (Louisville, KY: Westminster John Knox, 2009), 48–49. In this work, Evans is responsible for the chapter on Jesus's burial, and Wright the chapter on Jesus's Resurrection. Accordingly, I will credit each in the body of the text for their respective chapters.
5. Evans and Wright, *Jesus, the Final Days*, 44.
6. Ibid., 43–44.
7. Ibid., 70.
8. By Jesus's day, this passage was understood with reference to crucifixion because of its widespread usage (see Evans and Wright, *Jesus, the Final Days*, 29).
9. *Jewish War* 4.317, cited in Evans and Wright, *Jesus, the Final Days*, 61, emphasis added.
10. See Gary M. Burge and Gene L. Green, *The New Testament in Antiquity: A Survey of the New Testament Within Its Cultural Contexts*, 2nd ed. (Grand Rapids, MI: Zondervan Academic, 2020), 176, and Evans and Wright, *Jesus, the Final Days*, 53–54. Many other burial remains that have been uncovered could be from those who were crucified. The fact that we know the situation with Yehohanan is pure happenstance—because the nail "fishhooked" and couldn't be removed from his heel. Since many crucified victims were tied to the cross, there's no way to know definitively how some of these people died (see Evans and Wright, *Jesus, the Final Days*, 58–59).
11. Evans and Wright, *Jesus, the Final Days*, 64. While allowing for burial was not standard Roman practice everywhere for crucified victims, all signs point to it being the standard practice among Jews during peacetime, especially around Jerusalem (ibid., 62–64). The practice was necessarily different during the Jewish-Roman war of AD 66–70 and the subsequent siege of Jerusalem in AD 69–70 (ibid., 60–61). Evans writes: "The Gospel narrative is completely in step with Jewish practice, which Roman authorities during peacetime respected" (ibid., 69). See also Craig A. Evans, "Getting the Burial Traditions and Evidences Right," in *How God Became Jesus: The Real Origins of Belief in Jesus's Divine Nature* (Grand Rapids, MI: Zondervan, 2014), 71–93.
12. *Phaedo*, 64a–d, 67d–68c, cited in *Plato: Five Dialogues*, 101, 104–5.
13. Anthony J. Tomasino, *Judaism Before Jesus: The Events & Ideas That Shaped the New Testament World* (Downers Grove, IL: InterVarsity, 2003), 166–73.
14. See Evans and Wright, *Jesus, the Final Days*, 89–90.
15. Ibid., 91, emphasis added. See N. T. Wright, *The Resurrection of the Son of God* (Minneapolis, MN: Fortress, 2003), 557–63.

16. Evans and Wright, *Jesus, the Final Days*, 92. See Wright, *The Resurrection of the Son of God*, 558, for a discussion of the messianic movements surrounding Simon bar-Giora (which collapsed after the destruction of Jerusalem in AD 70) and Simeon bar-Kochba (sometimes spelled "Simon bar Kokhba") (which fell apart after the Romans put down the Jewish revolt of the mid-130s AD).

17. Evans and Wright, *Jesus, the Final Days*, 93. See Wright, *The Resurrection of the Son of God*, 559: "A moment's disciplined historical imagination . . . is enough to make the point. Jewish beliefs about a coming Messiah, and about the deeds such a figure would be expected to accomplish, came in various shapes and sizes, but they did not include a shameful death which left the Roman empire celebrating its usual victory."

18. Evans and Wright, *Jesus, the Final Days*, 102.

19. Ibid., 104. See Wright, *The Resurrection of the Son of God*, 709–10: "We are left with the secure historical conclusion: the tomb was empty, and various 'meetings' took place not only between Jesus and his followers (including at least one initial skeptic) but also, in at least one case (that of Paul; possibly, too, that of James), between Jesus and people who had not been among his followers. *I regard this conclusion as coming in the same sort of category, of historical probability so high as to be virtually certain, as the death of Augustus in AD 14 or the fall of Jerusalem in AD 70*" (ibid., 710, emphasis added).

20. Still, someone may balk and say (in the tradition of David Hume, 1711–1776), what is more likely—someone rose from the dead, or something quirky has happened with the accounts? While the believer may insist that the skeptic is left with no real explanation for the rise of Christian faith, the skeptic may be more comfortable with this lack of explanation than accepting the supernatural occurrence of the Resurrection. Here, again, is where we must acknowledge the paramount significance of background assumptions and ultimately our existential posture of faith. Indeed, the believer—especially the apologist—must leave room for the personal and existential act of faith; at some point, the *choice* to take the *risk* of faith. This is a significant ingredient in coming to faith in Jesus Christ and embracing his Resurrection from the dead. This assent of faith is reasonable; but there's always a way out if one wants it badly enough.

21. However, this is often the case for different reasons. Secular historical Jesus scholars frequently assume that Jesus was an apocalyptic prophet, announcing (and expecting) the imminent end of the cosmos. As such, there is no time for the age of the Church, since the end of all things is said to be immediately at hand. Géza Vermes, of a Jewish background, represents this perspective well: "Let it be re-stated for a last time, if [Jesus] meant and believed what he preached . . . namely, that the eternal Kingdom of God was truly at hand, *he simply could not have entertained the idea of founding and setting in motion an organized society intended to endure for ages to come*" (cited in Pitre,

Jesus and the Last Supper, 23, emphasis added). From the Protestant side, this thinking is often due to a subtle form of antisemitism, along the following lines: The Jews were obsessed with their priestly and religious rituals, seeing such religiosity as a means to sanctity; Jesus came to fix all that and show that the path to God is through *faith*, accessible *spiritually*—and not by any visible or ritual means. So, the Protestant view, historically, stems from an antisacramental bias—God is accessible spiritually, not through the mediation of physical signs (e.g., the sacraments). From this it follows that the true nature of the Church is *invisible* and *spiritual* (not visible and sacramental in the Catholic sense).

9. Did Jesus Found a Church?

1. Sometimes one hears Christian song lyrics that pit "relationship" and "religion" against each other; this is an expression of what we're talking about.

2. The problem, however, is the scattering of the northern tribes, noted above. Since they have largely been intermingled with the various nations, this regathering of all twelve tribes appears impossible—*unless one simultaneously gathers the nations*. But that has been precisely the divine plan all along (see Genesis 12:2–3; 22:16, 18).

3. See Josephus, *Antiquities*, 10.267, and St. Jerome, *Commentary on Daniel*, prologue.

4. See Josephus, *Antiquities*, 10.276; see also 2 Baruch 12:10 and 4 Ezra 39:5. See Pitre, *The Case for Jesus*, 107, 112. While modern interpreters often identify Daniel's four beasts as Babylon, Medes, Persians, and Greece, this was not how the vision was interpreted in Jewish and Christian antiquity. Two points in favor of the ancient interpretation are as follows: *Historically*, the Medes never ruled over the Jews independently of the Persians after Babylon (the Medes were incorporated into the Persian empire by 550 BC, more than a decade before Babylon fell to the Persians in 539 BC); and *literarily*, the book of Daniel consistently associates the "Medes and the Persians" together as one unified power (see Daniel 5:28; 6:8, 12, 15; 8:20). See *Ignatius Catholic Study Bible: Old and New Testament*, ed. Scott Hahn, co-ed. Curtis Mitch (San Francisco: Ignatius Press, 2024), 1,455.

5. The other place in the Old Testament where the equivalent of "kingdom of God" is used is in 1 Chronicles 28:5 and 2 Chronicles 13:5, 8. In both places "kingdom of the Lord [YHWH]" is used to refer to the Davidic Kingdom.

6. This *al bayit* in Isaiah 22 seems to have been understood in a priestly way as well in Jewish tradition. This would be very significant because Jesus would then be casting Peter not only in a royal administrative role but in a *priestly* one as well. See G. K. Beale, *The Temple and the Church's Mission: A Biblical Theology of the Dwelling Place of God* (Downers Grove, IL: InterVarsity, 2004), 188, and Michael Patrick Barber, "Jesus as Davidic Temple Builder

and Peter's Priestly Role in Matthew 16:16-19," *Journal of Biblical Literature* 132, no. 4 (2013): 935–53.

7. See Marcellino D'Ambrosio and Andrew Swafford, *What We Believe: The Beauty of the Catholic Faith* (West Chester, PA: Ascension Press, 2022), 138–39.

8. See Andrew D. Swafford, "Messianic Banquet and the Christian Proclamation," in *Hope and Death: Christian Responses*, ed. Michael A. Dauphinais and Roger W. Nutt (Steubenville, OH: Emmaus Academic, 2022), 19–34.

9. *Letter to the Ephesians*, ch. 20, cited in *Ignatius of Antioch and Polycarp of Smyrna*, 90.

10. Swafford, "Messianic Banquet," in *Hope and Death*, 32–33.

11. Brant Pitre, *Jesus and the Jewish Roots of Eucharist: Unlocking the Secrets of the Last Supper* (New York: Doubleday, 2011), 118–22.

12. See Pitre, *Jesus and the Last Supper*, 18–20.

13. See ibid., 129: "Jesus's words over the bread and wine at the Last Supper are not just evocative of the covenant sacrifices at Mount Sinai, but also of the bread (and wine) of the presence that is instituted by Moses in the Pentateuch as the symbolic and sacrificial memorial of the covenant sacrifice and a kind of earthly participation in the heavenly theophanic banquet."

14. Swafford, "Messianic Banquet," in *Hope and Death*, 33. In the words of Brant Pitre, "*[H]e is deliberately instituting a new Passover ritual that he expects the apostles to reenact after his death*" (*Jesus and the Last Supper*, 420, emphasis in original).

15. The passage in Exodus 24:8 where Moses speaks of the "blood of the covenant" features both of these words in the Greek Old Testament: "Behold the blood of the covenant [*diathekes*, a form of *diatheke*] which the Lord has made [*dietheto*, a form of diatithemi] with you" (Ex 24:8). Thus, here we have the verbal and nominal form of the Greek words featured in this passage in Luke's gospel, both used here in Exodus to describe the making of a covenant.

16. See Scott W. Hahn, "Christ, Kingdom, and Creation: Davidic Christology and Kingdom Ecclesiology in Luke-Acts," *Letter & Spirit* 3 (2007): 113–38, here 131–32. See also Scott W. Hahn, *Kinship by Covenant: A Canonical Approach to the Fulfillment of God's Saving Promises* (New Haven, CT: Yale University Press, 2009), 226–28.

17. Pitre, *Jesus and the Last Supper*, 512, emphasis added.

18. Pitre, *Jesus and the Jewish Roots of the Eucharist*, 145.

19. See Hahn, *Kinship by Covenant*, 229, 236–37.

10. The Difference Jesus Makes

1. Lewis, *Mere Christianity*, 122, emphasis in original.
2. Ibid., emphasis added.
3. Ibid.

4. Ibid., 128, first emphasis in original, second emphasis added.

5. Lewis, *The Screwtape Letters*, 70.

6. Pitre, *Introduction to the Spiritual Life*, 65–69.

7. See D'Ambrosio and Swafford, *What We Believe*, 150–53.

8. Lewis, *Mere Christianity*, 86.

9. Ibid., emphasis added.

10. See Philip Jenkins, *Hidden Gospels: How the Search for Jesus Lost Its Way* (Oxford: Oxford University Press, 2001), 3–26.

11. Lewis, *Mere Christianity*, 87.

12. See J. R. R. Tolkien, *The Hobbit: or There and Back Again* (Boston, MA: Houghton Mifflin Harcourt, 2012), 3–26.

13. See Jonathan T. Pennington, *The Sermon on the Mount and Human Flourishing: A Theological Commentary* (Grand Rapids, MI: Baker Academic, 2017), 43–47. See also Amy-Jill Levine, *Sermon on the Mount: A Beginner's Guide to the Kingdom of Heaven* (Nashville, TN: Abingdon, 2020), 52–53.

14. See *ST* II–IIae, q. 9, a. 4. See also *Thomas Aquinas: Commentary on the Beatitudes*, trans. John C. Graham (Coppell, TX, 2023), 21–22.

15. Pope Benedict XVI, *Jesus of Nazareth*, vol. 1, *From the Baptism in the Jordan to the Transfiguration*, trans. Adrian Walker (New York: Doubleday, 2007), 86, emphasis added.

16. Dale Allison, *The Sermon on the Mount* (Redwood City, CA: PublishDrive, 1999), 104–5.

17. See Pennington, *The Sermon on the Mount and Human Flourishing*, 71–76. *Teleios* is related to *telos*, the Greek word discussed earlier, meaning "end" or "goal."

18. *Veritatis Splendor* 12.

19. *Veritatis Splendor* 7.

20. *Confessions* 1.18, cited in *The Confessions*, trans. Boulding, 29.

21. This scene is reminiscent of another great reconciliation scene, namely, that between Jacob and Esau. After many years have passed (approximately twenty since Jacob's betrayal of Esau), Jacob is apprehensive at the prospect of meeting his brother again. And then surprisingly, we read this: "Esau ran to meet him, and embraced him, and fell on his neck and kissed him, and they wept" (Gn 33:4). In Genesis, this scene anticipates the later reconciliation between Joseph and his brothers after another devastating account of family betrayal (see Genesis 45:4–5; 50:20).

22. Pope Benedict, *Jesus of Nazareth*, 205–6.

23. *Confessions* 8.8, cited in *The Confessions*, trans. Boulding, 215.

24. Ibid.

25. *Confessions* 8.10, cited ibid., 218, emphasis added.

26. See *Confessions* 8.2–8.6, cited in *The Confessions*, trans. Boulding, 197–212.

27. *Confessions* 8.7, cited ibid., 212, emphasis added.

28. Lewis, *The Screwtape Letters*, 73.
29. *De Spiritu et Littera*, 19, 34, cited from *Veritatis Splendor*, 23.
30. See Pope Benedict, *Jesus of Nazareth*, 201.
31. *Salvifici Doloris* 25.
32. *Salvifici Doloris* 28 and 29.
33. See *Against Heresies* 3.17.3 and Anthony Giambrone, *Sacramental Charity, Creditor Christology, and the Economy of Salvation in Luke's Gospel* (Tübingen, Germany: Mohr Siebeck, 2017), 203.
34. Ibid.
35. See John Barclay, *Paul & the Gift* (Grand Rapids, MI: Eerdmans, 2015), 63, 472, 492.
36. Early Christians were especially known for their charity, in contrast to their pagan counterparts. See Rodney Stark, *The Rise of Christianity: How the Obscure, Marginal Jesus Movement Became the Dominant Religious Force in the Western World in a Few Centuries* (San Francisco: HarperCollins, 1997), 73–94.
37. *Love and Responsibility*, 80.

11. Growing in the Spiritual Life: Chastity, Forgiveness, and Faith

1. For those who have lost a loved one to suicide, in light of this teaching, there is no reason to lose hope (and there is very good reason to believe that our loved one's culpability is drastically diminished). We entrust them to the infinite mercy of God, who knows all the particulars about which we are so often in the dark (e.g., their internal state in their final moments).
2. Lewis, *Mere Christianity*, 91.
3. Ibid., emphasis added.
4. See Sayer, *Jack: A Life of C. S. Lewis*, 67–68.
5. Lewis, *Mere Christianity*, 99, emphasis added.
6. *Confessions* 8.7, cited in *The Confessions*, trans. Boulding, 213, emphasis added; Lewis, *Mere Christianity*, 99.
7. Lewis, *Mere Christianity*, 101, emphasis added.
8. Ibid., emphasis added.
9. Ibid., 101.
10. Ibid., emphasis added.
11. Ibid., 101–2.
12. *Confessions* 8.11, cited in *The Confessions*, trans. Boulding, 221.
13. *Confessions* 8.11, cited in *The Confessions*, trans. Boulding, 222.
14. See Wojtyła, *Love and Responsibility*, 150–57.
15. See Robert D. Enright, *Forgiveness Is a Choice: A Step-by-Step Process for Resolving Anger and Restoring Hope* (Washington, DC: American Psychological Association, 2001), 23–26, 28–29, 30–31, 135–36. Interestingly, as a long-practicing psychologist, Enright states: "Although a single painful event can lead to intense resentment, *most smoldering resentments are caused by*

a series of small offenses" (ibid., 49, emphasis added). Enright offers a principle that—even though one can think of exceptions—is on the whole worth taking into the depths of prayer (especially the second half of the statement): "A good rule to follow is that if you feel terribly guilty, you probably were at fault, *and if you feel completely innocent and absolutely justified in your anger, there is a good possibility that you may not be.* At some point in the forgiveness process, you may want to seek forgiveness for the wrongs you have done, even if your wrongs are 1% of the problem and the other person's wrongs are 99% of the problem" (ibid., 89, emphasis added).

16. Lewis, *Mere Christianity*, 118, emphasis added.
17. See Joseph Grenny, Kerry Patterson, Ron McMillan, Al Switzler, and Emily Gregory, *Crucial Conversations: Tools for Talking When Stakes Are High*, 3rd ed. (New York: McGraw-Hill, 2022), 78–104.
18. Lewis, *Mere Christianity*, 139.
19. Ibid.
20. Ibid.
21. Ibid., 140.
22. Ibid., emphasis added.
23. Ibid., 141.
24. Ibid.
25. Ibid., emphasis added.
26. Ibid.
27. See James Clear, *Atomic Habits: An Easy and Proven Way to Build Good Habits and Break Bad Ones* (London: Random House, 2018), 201.

12. *Mere* Catholicism: From the Trinity to the Eucharist—and Martyrdom

1. Lewis, *Mere Christianity*, 155.
2. Ibid., 156.
3. Matthias Joseph Scheeben, *The Mysteries of Christianity*, trans. Cyril Vollert (St. Louis, MO, 1946), 738.
4. John Paul II, homily, Peubla, Mexico, January 28, 1979.
5. Lewis, *Mere Christianity*, 157. Importantly, these are *eternal* relations within the Trinity, which means there never was a "time" when the Son and the Spirit did not exist—even though there is a hierarchy in their relations of origin (that is, the language referring to the First, Second, and Third Persons of the Trinity is meaningful—even though these are not *temporal* relations). Consequently, we must remove the time element from the "begetting" (or processions) within the Trinity.
6. Scheeben, *The Mysteries of Christianity*, 142.
7. See Lewis, *Mere Christianity*, 181. Also see *Gaudium et Spes* 22: "For, by his incarnation, he, the Son of God, has in a certain way united himself with

each individual." Cited in *Vatican Council II: Constitutions, Decrees, Declarations*, ed. Austin Flannery (New York: Costello, 1996), 185.

8. Lewis, *Mere Christianity*, 159. His analogy here calls to mind his *Chronicles of Narnia: The Lion, the Witch, and the Wardrobe*, where Aslan *breathes* on the characters who have been made statues by the White Witch and brings them back to life. See C. S. Lewis, *The Lion, the Witch, and the Wardrobe* (New York: Scholastic, 1950), 164–74. It also calls to mind Ezekiel's prophecy of dry bones receiving the "spirit" of God and coming to life (see Ezekiel 37:1–11). Note that the same Hebrew word (*ruach*) lies behind the English translations of "breath" and "spirit," thus connecting the prophecy of the gift of the Spirit in Ezekiel 36 (see 36:26–27) with the breath/spirit that brings the dry bones to life in Ezekiel 37.

9. See Andrew D. Swafford, "St. Paul in Matthias Scheeben: The Plenary Significance of the Incarnation," *Letter & Spirit* 11 (2016): 141–58.

10. See Lewis, *Mere Christianity*, 177, and Scheeben, *Mysteries of Christianity*, 245.

11. Lewis, *Mere Christianity*, 199.

12. Scheeben, *Mysteries of Christianity*, 485, 489, emphasis added.

13. Ibid., 493–94, emphasis added.

14. See ibid., 494–95.

15. See his *Letter to the Romans*, chapter 4, cited in *Ignatius of Antioch and Polycarp of Smyrna*, 115. Fittingly, he speaks of his imminent martyrdom in Eucharistic terms. "Permit me to be food for the beasts . . . I am the *wheat of God . . . the pure bread of Christ*" (ibid., 114, emphasis added).

16. See John Bergsma and Brant Pitre, *A Catholic Introduction to the Bible: The Old Testament* (San Francisco: Ignatius Press, 2018), 208.

17. At Mass, the priest (quietly) alludes to this passage, when he prays, "With humble spirit and contrite heart may we be accepted by you, O Lord, and may our sacrifice in your sight this day be pleasing to you, Lord God." The Latin text of the prayer shows direct connections to the Latin Vulgate version of this passage in Daniel 3. In Latin, the priest's prayer reads as follows (with the connections between the priest's prayer and Daniel 3 in bold): "*In spiritu humilitatis et in animo contrite suscipiamur a te, Domine: et sic fiat sacrificium nostrum in conspectu tuo hodie, ut placeat tibi, Domine Deus.*" Here is the Latin Vulgate's version of Daniel 3 (again, with the connections to the Mass prayer in bold): "*Et non est in tempore hoc princeps, et dux, et propheta, neque holocaustum, neque sacrificium, neque oblatio, neque incensum, neque locus primitiarum coram te, ut possimus invenire misericordiam tuam, sed in animo **contrito**, et spiritu humilitatis suscipiamur. Sicut in holocausto arietum, et taurorum, et sicut in millibus agnorum pinguium, **sic fiat sacrificium nostrum in conspectu tuo hodie, ut placeat tibi**.*" This connection is significant because it draws together liturgical sacrifice, martyrdom, and the Mass—with reference to both the

making present of Christ's sacrifice and our entering into this paschal sacrifice through the liturgy of the Mass.

18. See *Salvifici Doloris* 19: "Christ has also raised human suffering to the level of Redemption. Thus each man, in his suffering, can also become a sharer in the redemptive suffering of Christ." St. John Paul II continues: "In this dimension—the dimension of love—the Redemption which has already been completely accomplished is, in a certain sense, constantly being accomplished. Christ achieved the Redemption completely and to the very limit; but at the same time He did not bring it to a close. . . . Yes, it seems to be part of the very essence of Christ's redemptive suffering that this suffering requires to be unceasingly completed" (ibid., 24).

19. Matthew Ramage, *The Experiment of Faith: Pope Benedict XVI on Living the Theological Virtues in a Secular Age* (Washington, DC: Catholic University of America Press, 2020), 257. He recounts his suffering on pp. 255–56.

13. Does Christianity Really Work?

1. D'Ambrosio and Swafford, *What We Believe*, 126.
2. Lewis, *Mere Christianity*, 210.
3. Ibid., emphasis added.
4. Andrew and Sarah Swafford, *Gift and Grit*, 15–18.
5. See Lewis, *The Screwtape Letters*, 65.
6. G. K. Chesterton, *What's Wrong with the World* (Manchester, NH: Sophia Institute Press, 2021), 31, emphasis added.
7. See Ramage, *The Experiment of Faith*, 264–66.

Andrew Swafford is a professor of theology at Benedictine College. He is the author of *A Catholic Guide to the New Testament* and coauthor with his wife, Sarah Swafford, of *Gift and Grit: How Heroic Virtue Can Change Your Life and Relationships*. He also coauthored *What We Believe: The Beauty of the Catholic Faith* with Marcellino D'Ambrosio.

Swafford holds a doctor of sacred theology degree from the University of St. Mary of the Lake and a master's degree in Old Testament and Semitic languages from Trinity Evangelical Divinity School. He has spoken at numerous conferences, including the National Catholic Youth Conference (NCYC), the National Eucharistic Congress, RENEW Toronto, and the Defending the Faith Conference in Steubenville, Ohio.

He is the general editor of and a contributor to *The Great Adventure Catholic Bible*. An avid student of Brazilian jiu-jitsu, he lives in Atchison, Kansas, with Sarah and their children.

Website: theswaffords.com
X: @andrew_swafford

Founded in 1865, Ave Maria Press, a ministry of the Congregation of Holy Cross, is a Catholic publishing company that serves the spiritual and formative needs of the Church and its schools, institutions, and ministers; Christian individuals and families; and others seeking spiritual nourishment.

For a complete listing of titles from

Ave Maria Press

Sorin Books

Forest of Peace

Christian Classics

visit www.avemariapress.com